The Fight of Faith

The Fight of Faith

Lives and Testimonies from the Battlefield

Compiled and Edited by
Michael Claydon and Philip Bray

Panoplia Publishing

Published by Panoplia Publishing
Flat 3, 415 Archway Road, LONDON, N6 4HT

www.thefightoffaith.org

The Fight of Faith
Copyright © 2013 Panoplia Publishing

ISBN 978-0-9576089-0-0

Typeset in 11 Point Sabon by Rickfords Hill Publishing Ltd.

Printed and bound in China by 1010 Printing International Ltd.

Contents

List of Illustrations

Diagrams

Foreword

The notion that Christians can serve in the Armed Forces is a surprise to many in every generation. While this is partly a misunderstanding of the teaching from the Sermon on the Mount, it is perhaps confusing to some that a profession which may involve the deployment of violent action should be occupied by those who have an eternal indebtedness to Christ's Gospel of Love. This unbalanced view of the Gospel – for in truth it should balance God's righteousness as well as His love in perfect proportion – needs to be corrected with Biblical evidence.

Although military force has often been grossly abused, there are at least four reasons why this is not invariably the case. If the cause is just, the outcome predictable, and the means used proportional to restore peace, Christians may participate in the military profession with a calm conscience.

First, the Bible reveals that devoted men were involved in military operations. In the Old Testament, Abraham, Joshua, Gideon, and King David are all examples. The Writer to the Hebrews refers with approval in Chapter 11 of his Epistle to those who '…from weakness were made strong, became mighty in war, put foreign armies to flight.' The four Centurions mentioned in the New Testament emerge from the account in glowing terms. The Centurion whose servant the Lord Jesus healed, the Centurion who recognised Jesus' divinity at the Cross, Cornelius, in whose home the first Gentile Church was formed, and Julius, who escorted the Apostle Paul to Rome, are all presented as honourable, caring, and responsible leaders. There is no indication that any of them forsook their profession or were required to do so.

Secondly, if the evidence ended here, the conclusion that Christians may serve in the Armed Forces would be open to the charge that it was based on silence. However, it is reinforced by the fact that the Christian life is likened to a number of professions in

Scripture of which the soldier is one (Ephesians 6 and 2 Timothy 2 etc). The Holy Spirit would never have inspired this illustration if the profession was invariably dishonourable.

Thirdly, the New Testament acknowledges the part that human government has to play in the maintenance of law and order and in Romans 13 we are reminded that this responsibility may involve the use of a degree of force when necessary.

There is, however, a fourth and significant piece of evidence to justify the holding of the military profession by Christian people, and this is the theme of this book. Numerous Christians can testify to the Lord's sustaining power when involved in military operations. Promises from Scripture have been brought to mind at apposite moments and prayers have been answered. An almost unexpected inner peace has been experienced and enjoyed (and that is often an appropriate description!) at times of pressure. The Lord never forsakes those who are forgiven and reconciled to Him. The subjects of these chapters proved the power of God to keep as well as to save a man.

These brief biographical accounts cover a wide range of circumstances geographically, historically, and in the level of responsibility held by their subjects. However, all knew 'the joy of sins forgiven' and proved the Lord to be faithful in their professional responsibilities. The editors, whose vision and diligence have brought this book into being, and the writers will surely have prayed that a younger generation will draw encouragement from these accounts and, where necessary, be given the grace to emulate their Christian military forebears.

Ian Dobbie
Sevenoaks   May 2013

Preface and Acknowledgements

While serving in the Armed Forces we have had the privilege of meeting individuals and reading many instances that illustrate the goodness and truth of the Lord Jesus Christ. It seemed good to us to collect these accounts into a single book.

Therefore, this book contains a mix of styles which, while we have tried to remove any great differences in structure, we have retained in order to allow each chapter to tell its unique story. We have been pleased that the *Special Relationship*, which has been of such military importance over the years, is again illustrated in, and we trust might also be strengthened by, these chapters. But equally thrilling is that, while the chapters are fundamentally about war, two wondrous themes have emerged.

First is the peace that comes through the effect of the reign of the Lord Jesus Christ in individuals' lives. The subjects are from several different nationalities and periods of history – and even opposing sides in the same war – yet all speak of having received the same free gift of salvation through simple faith in Jesus Christ.

Secondly, it has been humbling to consistently see the willingness of the authors and all those who have in some way contributed to this book to do so at no cost for the simple reason that they have freely and undeservedly received so much from God and are willing to give it freely to others. This in itself is evidence that the words that they write are true.

Therefore, we wish to thank the following people: the authors for generously contributing their chapters; an advisory panel who have given so much time and help over this past year; John Hildred for translating Siegfried Schäfer's chapter; Jonathan Kitchen of Jonathan Kitchen Photography, and Rickfords Hill Publishing for professional assistance; the publishers, Thomas Nelson, Evangelical Press, and Christian Focus who have kindly granted permission to publish some of their material; the Moody Bible Institute Archives for researching and providing at no cost images to support Chapter 7; and, finally, the Imperial War Museum and the National Army Museum of London for providing the excellent images (listed on pages 6 – 9).

But, above all, thanks be to God for 'His indescribable gift,' which we commend to you in this brief series of lives and testimonies from the world's battlefields.

The Editors
London   May 2013

1

Called to Be a Soldier for Christ

By Reverend Major Joe Mullins MC

Field Marshal Arthur Wellesley, Duke of Wellington said 'All the business of war and indeed all the business of life, is to endeavour to find out what you don't know by what you do. That's what I call, "guessing what was at the other side of the hill."'

A gushing lady came up to the Duke following one of his victories in battle saying, 'What a glorious thing must be a victory, sir.' The Duke responded, 'The greatest tragedy in the world, madam, except a defeat.' In other words, violent confrontation is a sad and bad business by any standard, yet it is also true that those involved with a good conscience learn many lessons about human nature and leadership, which stand them in good stead for the rest of their lives. It was certainly so with me.

When I was born at Chevington Grove, near Bury St Edmunds, my father was serving in the Finance Department of the Anglo-Egyptian Sudan, as it was known then, in Khartoum. Since my mother had already borne my elder sister, Jean, a nanny was engaged to assist this temporarily single mum. My father came back to England when I was quite small. I think I was a bit of a handful!

When I was found by the Saviour at an Easter Scripture Union camp at the age of seventeen it was borne in on me that my conversion to Christ was due more to 'Nannie Martley's' prayers than perhaps any other single factor. I still have a vivid impression of her gracious face after all these years, though the last time I saw her was on a visit when I was six.

I went out to Kenya as a student farmer under John Etherington's oversight after leaving school at eighteen. I enjoyed the open-air life in the Kenya Highlands and was there when the Second World War broke out in September 1939.

Returning to Britain, I enlisted in the 5th Special Reserve Battalion, Scots Guards, equipped with skis and windproof clothing for Arctic conditions. The proposed expeditionary force to assist the Finns against Russia was mercifully aborted. After the Royal

Military College, Sandhurst, I was commissioned as a 2nd Lieutenant in the Queen's Royal Regiment, West Surreys, in October 1940.

In August 1942, I joined the 1st Battalion in Peshawar, which was then the capital of the North-West Frontier Province of India, now Pakistan.

We moved steadily eastwards and, after jungle training, joined the 33rd Brigade of the 7th Indian Division in the Arakan, now Bangladesh. After being surrounded by the Japanese invaders and fighting our way out in February/March 1944, we were flown up to Assam to meet the far larger Japanese force coming through the Naga Hills. There are incidents in the Arakan campaign which are still indelibly imprinted on my mind: ...night patrols... Christian fellowship in a dugout... Christmas mail and dinner... roast duck delivered by parachute air drops! Now an acting Captain, I had taken over command of B Company in the Arakan from Major John Hamilton, who was badly wounded. I was 23.

After the fall of Kohima in May 1944, the 33rd Corps of the 14th Army advanced over the Naga Hills, amid monsoon downpours, supplied by parachute airdrops from the brave Dakotas. I was promoted Acting Major with effect from 28th April 1945.

We advanced successfully down through Burma with motorised columns, and light armoured tanks led by infantry. After taking the town of Prome on the River Irrawaddy we were switched across the central hills to Pegu to cut off the retreating Japanese force, who were making for an escape route across the Sittang River to endeavour to reach Thailand.

We were badly depleted in numbers, largely due to malaria and dysentery. The monsoon was full-on and, sloshing through the paddy fields, we were beset by leeches by day and foot rot and hungry mosquitoes by night. The 1st Queens were reduced to A and B Companies with 60 men each, instead of 120 each.

We occupied a village called Letpanthonbyn and were ordered to do a night-fighting patrol to cut the Pegu-Martaban rail line, along which the retreating Japanese were believed to be marching. We left only a skeleton force in the village. Balancing on slippery paddy *bunds* in the dark was no joke. We did not succeed in finding the enemy that night.

Returning very weary the next morning, we were confronted with the news that a Japanese force was now in occupation of our village. We received orders from Brigade Headquarters to retake the village immediately. After rest and food, our Battalion Commander, Colonel John Terry, made a battle plan. A Company on the right and B Company (my company) on the left were to advance and drive out the enemy, who were dug in behind a mud bank reservoir.

The attack was delayed till the afternoon for two reasons: the extreme weariness of the troops and some misdirected artillery fire, causing casualties to A Company. B Company, under my command, was to put in the final attack with covering fire from A Company on the right. All went well till we approached the reservoir, before which was a clearing, interspersed with bushy mango trees and a Buddhist Temple to the right, opposite A Company (see Battle diagram).

I took up a position behind the trunk of a mango tree to direct the attack. Attacking across the open field with bayonets fixed, we came under heavy fire from automatic weapons behind the reservoir bank. Driven back, we tried to encircle the Japanese positions from the left (see diagram) but again came under heavy fire.

Returning to a frontal position, we tried to reach the reservoir bank but were repulsed again. Tiny Taylor, my second-in-command, was wounded, and also my runner. Crouching behind the large mango tree, I called up Sergeant Everett and two other seasoned men and shared with them my plan to crawl across A Company's front and round the Buddhist temple, which afforded cover, to reach the bank of the reservoir on the east side. I feared an enemy counter-attack after dark if we did not dislodge them. I had no orders from Headquarters, except to drive the enemy out. So as dusk fell we set off with what ammo and grenades we could muster (see dotted line). It dawned on us that we four alone were confronting an unknown number of fanatical Japanese fighters. Reserving the remainder of our ammo for what might be a last-ditch stand, we lay 'doggo' to see what might happen.

Sometime between two and three a.m. we heard a terrific commotion going on at the northern end of the reservoir. The Japanese were collecting up their ammo and equipment, jabbering away. They were obviously preparing to move, but where to? That was the question. Then, as the first streaks of light from the east lightened the sky, we could see men silhouetted, moving from left to right. Would they advance down the *bund* under which we were crouching or... ?

To our great relief and in answer to our prayers, we heard them sloshing out across the paddy fields to the east. We fired a few volleys

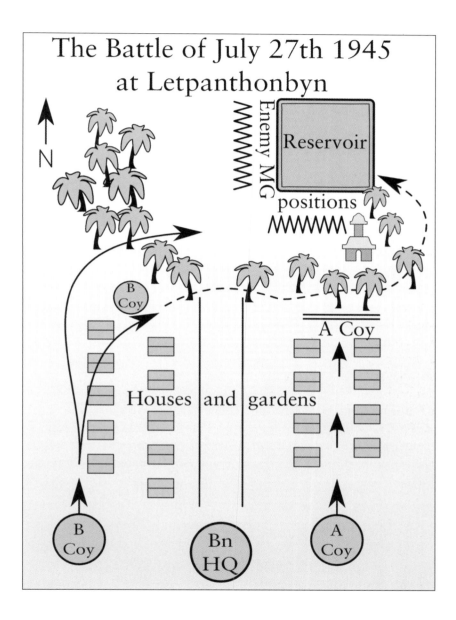

The Battle of July 27th 1945 at Letpanthonbyn

in the direction of their retreating steps, waited until the sun was above the horizon, then stealthily advanced to where the Japanese had been, fearing the possibility of an ambush. There was none. The problem now was this: as far as our Battalion was concerned we were missing, presumed dead. As far as they knew, the Japanese still occupied this end of the village. We did not want to be shot up by our own men, so we decided to walk back down the village 'street' singing army songs, like

Pack up your troubles in
your old kit bag and smile...

This we did and were greeted with wide-eyed amazement and then hugs. As I began to relax, I suddenly felt my steel helmet weighing a bit heavily. I took it off and felt the top of my head. Surprised to find a scratch, maybe half an inch to an inch long, I looked at the helmet. The foam rubber and leather crown were ripped to bits. I pulled them out, revealing two gaping holes and a dent where Japanese bullets had penetrated the steel and had been miraculously deflected from my head.

As I gazed at the helmet, it seemed that God was saying to me 'Joe, you've no right to be alive. Your only right to live is to give yourself back to Me.' We lost 25 men in that battle. I am ashamed to say that up to this point, like Peter, I had been 'follow[ing] Him at a distance.' I have looked at that helmet many times since and my heart has been full of repentance and thanksgiving.

Soon after the battle, I was hospitalised at Pegu with a sort of eczema on my legs as a result of leech bites and continually soggy boots and socks. In the muggy monsoon heat this took eight weeks to clear up, giving me plenty of time for the lesson to sink in and to reflect on what God wanted me to do with my life. 'Lord, what do you want me to do?' was my prayer. I was demobbed from the Army on 18th June 1946 at Aldershot, just before my 26th birthday.

How wonderfully God has guided me since then...Oxford... theological training...hockey Blue...ordination at St. Paul's Cathedral, London...two years in a London parish... called to India with the Scripture Union...met and married Edith Helen Gooding in 1956, the beginning of a wonderful partnership...twelve years pastoring at St John's, Bangalore...in 1974 emigrated to Australia with six wonderful kids...

It was a fairly traumatic business adjusting to Australia after twenty years in India. We kept thinking *'when are we going home to Bangalore?'* However, we survived and, 67 years on, Australia is home! I owe more to Edith, a wonderful wife and mother, than I can express. We rejoice to be in the business of exporting the Gospel as our Lord Jesus bade us. It is special that we are in touch with a Japanese family we met in Jakarta and a Burmese missionary, Philip Aung, who lives on the Thai-Burmese border and was raised near Letpanthonbyn!

> *How good is the God we adore,*
> *Our faithful, unchangeable Friend.*
> *Whose love is as great as His power,*
> *And knows neither measure nor end.*

The Revd Maj Joe Mullins MC, pictured above with the helmet in 2010, is now aged 92 and lives in Canberra, Australia. He kindly gave permission for this testimony to be included in the book.

2

The Road to Unafraid

How the Army's Top Ranger Faced Fear and Found Courage
through 'Black Hawk Down' and Beyond

*By US Army Major (Retired) Jeff Struecker
with Dean Merrill*

United States Army Rangers don't get scared. They have made a name for themselves as the fearless ones. They are a tough, disciplined, quick-strike force that parachutes or helicopters in to nasty situations, kicks down doors, captures the bad guys, and forces openings for the rest of the US Army to follow – hence their motto, 'Rangers Lead the Way.'

Give them the hardest, most dangerous, most challenging mission you can think of. They'll take it on. They are elite – fewer than half of one percent of all active-duty soldiers in the US Army are capable of serving in the 75th Ranger Regiment. They go where others are not able or not trained enough to go. They instinctively run *towards* the battle, not away from it.

At least that's the mystique. Line up any 100 guys who have served successfully in the Ranger Regiment and ask if they've ever been afraid. You'll get no takers.

They stand in the long, proud line of those Rangers who were the first souls on the beaches of Normandy on D-Day back in 1944. It was Rangers who scaled straight up the 90-foot cliffs of Pointe-du-Hoc that day to knock out a nest of 155mm German cannons that were holding off the Allied invasion.

It was Rangers who jumped onto the airfields of Grenada (1983), taking on the enemy with no backup for hours. We Rangers did the same in Panama (1989). We were the ones who came oh-so-close to breaking the back of Somali warlord Mohamed Farrah Aidid and restoring sanity to that desperate country (1993) – until the US government pulled us out. If you've read Mark Bowden's excellent bestseller, *Black Hawk Down,* or seen the Academy Award-winning movie you know all about that. In this chapter, I'll give you my take on what happened there.

* * *

It may surprise you, but I admit that I have been afraid more than once or twice during my more than twenty years as a US Army Ranger. That may upset some people, but it's true. I have felt the same fears as those who've never worn the uniform: fear of death, fear of losing one's most valued relationships, fear of running out of money, fear of getting sick, fear of failure, and fear of embarrassment. These happen all across the human spectrum.

How we handle our fears makes a huge difference. We can let them paralyse us or we can find the courage to rise above them. Through my experiences, you will see some extreme examples of facing threats and overcoming the panic they generate inside. I hope it gives you answers for the private battles you face.

However, there was another and greater fear, which I came to understand and to be delivered from when I was aged thirteen. At this age, I overcame a paralysing fear of death that dates back to my earliest memories. For most of my childhood I was terrified at thoughts of the afterlife. At the age of thirteen, my neighbours came to my house and described Jesus as the sinless Son of God. They explained how my sin separated me from God and demanded death

Major (Retired) Jeff Struecker pictured in Iraq during Operation IRAQI FREEDOM in 2003.

and hell. Though they could not possibly have known at the time, they also answered my greatest fears by describing Jesus' brutal death on the cross for the sake of my sin and His resurrection, which affords me the promise of eternal life in heaven with Him. Later that night, as I lay down in bed, I committed my life into the hands of Jesus and asked Him to take away my fear of death by giving me the promise that I would live with Him in heaven one day. The next morning when I woke, I had no fear of death.

A Small Problem

It was a Sunday afternoon in Mogadishu, but I can assure you nobody was taking a nap. Earlier thoughts about organising a volleyball game in the warm sun there at our Mogadishu airport compound by the ocean were long forgotten. Intelligence was now saying we had a golden opportunity to catch not one but two high aides to Mohamed Farrah Aidid, the warlord who was basically ruining Somalia.

This desert country on the tip of northeast Africa didn't have just a bad government in 1993; it had had *no* functioning government at all for two years. If you wanted to mail a letter, there was no postal system to accept or deliver it. If you had a child who needed schooling, there was no such public institution. If you were in trouble and needed a police officer to protect you, you'd better have a bribe ready. This demonstrates the truth of the exhortation in the Bible that the church is to pray for governments:

> *First of all, then, I urge that entreaties and prayers, petitions and thanksgivings, be made on behalf of all men, ... for kings and all who are in... authority, so that we may lead a tranquil and quiet life in all godliness and dignity.*[1]

The lack of good leadership in Somalia had a desperate effect on the people.

It was such a shame, because as I had looked around Mogadishu I could not help thinking it had the potential to be one of the world's great resort cities. The gentle breezes off the Indian Ocean, the sandy beaches, and the warm sunshine were all reminiscent of the French Riviera. Instead, it was currently shot to pieces, totally trashed, the most violent place on earth. Only the mosques seemed to have been spared. There was little evidence of anything of Christ.

Aidid and his competitors ran the country's daily life through sheer force, controlling the drug trade and choking off the world's food aid as soon as it arrived in the port. He had a sinister scheme for getting and keeping fighters. His policy was simple: 'Free drugs if you'll join my militia.' As a result, he had recruited thousands of desperate young men who stayed high much of the time. The average Somali lived in daily fear: more than 2 million had been driven from their homes and 300,000 had starved to death.

Then (in 1993) the United Nations commissioned us, along with troops from several other nations, to take care of this bully once and for all, ushering him towards a trial for crimes against humanity. In the two months *Task Force Ranger* had been here, we'd already conducted six raids into the dusty, chaotic city, nabbing key players

in Aidid's militia each time. Cooperative Somalis who wanted a better life for their country would feed us tips on where to look. Soon our small helicopters would swoop down from the sky to drop special operators on designated rooftops or in alleys nearby. They would kick in the doors, immediately throw flash-bang grenades to stun everyone inside, then handcuff them with plasticuffs before the targets knew what had hit them.

Meanwhile, Rangers were already arriving on the larger Black Hawk helicopters, which would hover 30 feet or so over each of the four corners of the block. Three-inch ropes would be flung downward and Rangers would slide down to the street like fire-fighters descending a station pole, a manoeuvre called *fast-roping*. The instant the Rangers hit the ground, they would take control of the intersection, thereby setting up a controlled perimeter that no one could penetrate.

This rectangle would stay in place until a column of vehicles rolled up to the door of the target building to load up the captured. This was normally my mission to lead. The Rangers at the four corners, upon receiving a radio signal, would fall back in our direction to join the convoy along with the special operators. We'd race out of the neighbourhood before most people even had a clue what was going down.

Two for the Price of One

One afternoon (3rd October 1993) we got word that a high-level meeting was under way at a certain three-storey building on Hawlwadig Road, just a block north of the Olympic Hotel. Sunday was a normal business day in this Muslim country; their day of worship is Friday. At this meeting, not one but *two* of the big shots were supposed to be present: Omar Salad, who was Aidid's top political adviser, and Abdi Hassan Awale Qeybdid, his interior minister. This was a lucky break.

It would have been nicer not to have to go in during the late afternoon, when crowds of people were around and paying attention. We'd rather have done this raid during the night or early morning, but the opportunity for a 'two-fer' was too good to pass up.

'Struecker, you know how to find this place?' Lieutenant Colonel Danny McKnight asked me as we stood in the JOC (Joint Operations

Centre). By studying satellite maps, I had become something of an expert in the geography of the city. It was a challenge, since no street signs existed and there was definitely no help to be had from MapQuest or Triple-A. However, gradually I had built up my memory bank of local landmarks and what streets led where.

'Yes, sir,' I replied. 'I have driven by there several times. It's just a few blocks east of the Bakara Market, which is not the most pleasant neighbourhood for us, as you know. But we can definitely get there.' This was the heart of Aidid territory, where open-air booths sold everything from cucumbers to rugs to rifles.

'Okay. We're moving out in ten minutes. Birds lift off first and you'll be heading up the road almost immediately after.' That was the way it usually ran for Ranger missions; we had to be ready to go on very short notice.

While the helicopters were loading up, I lined up the ground column at the gate. My Humvee (that's army-talk for *HMMWV* or *High Mobility Multi-Wheeled Vehicle*, the prototype of what eventually became *the Hummer* in today's auto-market) would lead the way, with young Private First Class Jeremy Kerr as my driver. He was getting all kinds of new experience here in Somalia: such as his first time driving a military vehicle or wearing night goggles. All this was a steep learning curve for Jeremy.

In the back, behind a metal bomb-protection plate, was Sergeant Dominick Pilla, the best machine gunner I'd ever seen. He was a big, funny guy from *New Joyzee* whose practical jokes and skits kept the entire battalion entertained. Beside him was young Specialist Tim Moynihan, a bongo-playing guy with thick black hair who could have grown a great-looking beard had regulations allowed. He was well-liked and popular among all the guys.

Up on top in the turret was Private First Class Brad Paulson manning the big .50-calibre machine gun. He was a small fellow from the Midwest who almost looked young enough to be in high school, except for his 'high-and-tight' military haircut. I thought of him as a kid brother.

Right behind our vehicle was the other half of our squad in a second Humvee, led by my right hand, Sergeant Danny Mitchell. His super-slow Arkansas drawl made some people assume he wasn't the sharpest knife in the drawer, but this was the opposite of the truth. I had soon come to realise he was qualified to fill in for me at any time. We'd worked together a long time and could almost read each other's minds. He was incredibly loyal and would do anything I asked.

Next came more Humvees and three five-ton flatbed trucks for holding lots of people, a total of twelve vehicles in all. I was the lead navigator, while Lieutenant Colonel McKnight, further back in a Humvee, would be calling the main plays.

We roared out of the gate as soon as the signal came that the helicopters, already in the air, were about to launch their assault. The distance to cover was no more than a four-minute drive into the sandy, garbage-littered streets of Mogadishu. We dodged burned-out vehicles along the way and swerved around piles of loose tyres, old furniture, and wood scraps that residents had set on fire to draw attention to previous gun battles. I found it odd that, instead of running away from trouble, the residents here almost seemed drawn to it, coming out of their crumbling houses to get in on the action.

As we got close to the hotel, I instructed Jeremy Kerr to turn right. Actually, I spoke a block or two too soon. It was the only wrong turn I took during my whole time in Somalia. The confusion was quickly remedied, however, and the whole convoy reassembled behind the hotel, a five-storey white building with lots of balconies, to await our next move.

We heard shots in the distance; it was clear that the Rangers at the four corners were taking fire from Aidid's hidden militia. They were not about to just let us capture their leaders unchallenged. Battered pickup trucks with their backs full of rifle-waving militia began screeching around corners.

However, at the target house things were progressing smoothly. The time for extracting the bad guys was almost here. The main point of this mission, getting the two men, was nearly wrapped up.

Just a Minute …

Then came the fateful moment when I first heard about a 'small problem.'

'Hey, Struecker, we've got a casualty,' came Danny McKnight's voice through the radio. 'You need to go get him, put him on your vehicle, and take him back to base.'

I got out and walked back to his Humvee. 'Sir, what's up?' I asked. 'What's going on?'

'I don't know who it is, but his condition doesn't sound too good. You need to get him out of here. I'll give you one of the cargo Humvees' (the military version of a pickup truck) 'and your two with your squad can escort him back to the airfield.'

'Who are we talking about, sir? And where is he?'

'I don't know the name, but he's one of the guys in Sergeant Eversmann's *chalk*' (combat team) 'just up ahead. You can ask Captain Steele if you want – he's right by the target building.'

The problem was this: as Eversmann's men had fast-roped down from their Black Hawk helicopter to secure the northwest corner of the perimeter, a young Ranger named Todd Blackburn had missed the rope as he jumped out. Either that, or he took a bullet into his Kevlar vest just then, which didn't penetrate, of course, but successfully stunned him right at the point of grabbing the rope. To make matters worse, the Black Hawk was higher than normal from the ground, in order to avoid some power lines on that corner (not that Mogadishu's electricity supply was even functioning anymore). Todd Blackburn had plunged some 70 feet and hit the street head first with a sickening thud.

I ran back to the convoy, grabbed a stretcher off the back of the cargo vehicle and hollered for Moynihan to follow me. When we got to Eversmann's corner, I immediately saw a medic working furiously on the guy in the street, trying to get his airway open. I moved to catch a glimpse of Blackburn's face and it was not a pretty sight.

He still had his helmet on; nobody wanted to remove it for fear of jarring him. 'He's hurt his back,' I said to myself. 'We're going to have to be really careful moving him.'

We gingerly lifted Blackburn onto the stretcher, then hoisted it up and started back down the street. As we ran, the enemy fire grew worse to the point that we had to take shelter for a moment. 'Man, these guys are coming from about every window and rooftop, aren't they?' I thought. I had hoped we could get this job done without rousing the whole militia.

In spite of the hammering we fought our way back to the vehicles, where we loaded Blackburn on the back of the cargo Humvee. A medic quickly went to work on him, completely exposed to the incoming fire. A special operator jumped aboard to fire back and to try to protect the medic and Todd.

After a quick consultation with Lieutenant Colonel McKnight to tell him I was leaving with three vehicles and to advise him on how the rest could find their way home without my map, we moved out. Turning right at the first corner, we headed for the next street, intending to make another right back towards the ocean and out of the city. 'We need to take it slow,' I instructed my guys, 'so we don't break Blackburn's neck. Dodge every pothole you can.'

At the second corner, however, it was as if the whole city opened up on us. As we threaded our way through the narrow street with two- and three-storey buildings on both sides, bullets were flying our way from every direction. We fought back with everything we had: our personal M-16s, submachine guns, and Paulson's .50 calibre up on top. The fighting was definitely intense.

We had stormed our way through about five blocks when we reached National Street, a four-lane boulevard. A right turn here would head us out of the slums and back towards the base. We were just rounding the corner when Dom Pilla spotted a gunman levelling his AK-47 right at him. Dom fired at the guy, who in the very same instant fired at Dom.

The next thing I knew, Moynihan was screaming in the back, 'Pilla's hit!'

I whirled to look around the corner of the metal plate. Dom Pilla had slumped over into Tim Moynihan's lap and there was blood everywhere. The whole back of the Humvee was bright red. I could not believe how much damage one bullet had caused.

'What do we do? Dom's killed!' Moynihan yelled. At this, my other two guys, Kerr and Paulson up on top, began freaking out as well. For a second I panicked on the inside. I had just lost a very good soldier, a man I was responsible for and a good friend. I swallowed hard. This operation was going seriously askew.

The Gauntlet

I could not let myself think more about all that. I had to detach myself and jump back into tactical mode. Otherwise, a horrible situation would get even worse. 'Take charge, Jeff,' I told myself.

'Moynihan,' I said in a steady voice, 'stop what you're doing. Take your weapon and face right; pick up Dominic's sector of fire.' He quietened down as he followed my order.

'Kerr, step on it!' I said to the driver. 'Fly down this road as fast as you can.' No more worrying about jostling Todd Blackburn's neck or back in the vehicle behind us: better that than any more of us getting killed in this maelstrom of hot lead. We could not afford to poke along as fat, easy targets in the middle of a hostile city.

We roared down National Street for a good mile until we came upon the big food distribution centre. Twice a day in Mogadishu, UNICEF, CARE, Food for the Hungry, and other agencies handed out relief and every starving Somali showed up to get their next meal. Wouldn't you know, this just happened to be the hour of the evening handout. The road was packed with literally thousands of people. I could not even see to the far side of the crowd. Meanwhile, we were still getting hammered from the buildings on both sides.

'Paulson!' I hollered up to my gunner. 'We've got to clear a path. Start shooting over their heads. Don't kill anybody, but make them think you're shooting at them so they'll scatter.' To help get the crowd's attention, I threw half a dozen flash-bang grenades.

The sea of humanity at the distribution centre started to part, slowly. 'Hurry up, people!' my driver yelled. The hail of bullets continued.

Finally, I could not stall any longer. 'Just floor it,' I told Kerr. 'They'll get out of the way.' We plunged towards the crowd and eventually reached the far side of it.

On our way again and building speed, the hostile fire slacked off a bit. Instead of getting shot at from 50 places at once it was down to five places at once. Just then, the voice of Platoon Sergeant Bob Gallagher, my direct superior on this particular mission, came on the radio: 'How things goin'?'

I definitely did not want to answer that. Most of our unit had heard about Blackburn's fall by now but almost nobody knew about Pilla and bad news has a way of messing with soldiers' minds, even highly-trained Rangers. I ignored the question.

Gallagher's voice came again: 'How's it goin,' Struecker?'

I could not stiff-arm him again. Finally I said, 'I don't want to talk about it.'

That reply, of course, only piqued his interest. 'You got any casualties?'

'Yeah, one.' 'Just let it go, man!' I pleaded inside my mind.

'Who is he, and what's his status?'

I took a deep breath. 'It's Pilla,' I finally answered.

'What's his status?'

Another breath. I was cornered. I had to answer the question: 'He's dead.' I immediately started to wonder about Pilla's faith. I only knew him as a good soldier and a Ranger buddy but I didn't know about his faith in Jesus Christ. I hoped in those few seconds that Dominic was with God in heaven through a relationship with Jesus Christ but I wasn't sure and that bothered me.

The radio, which had been crackling with lots of conversation all across the city between our various units, suddenly went quiet. Nobody said another word. Soldiers were simply stunned. This was the first man we'd lost since landing in Somalia. The invincible Ranger Regiment had been nicked by an untrained, impoverished Somali gunman with little more than a grudge to pursue.

I switched frequency on the radio and called the JOC back at the base. 'Hey, I'm about two minutes out. Get the surgeons ready for us, okay? I have got one guy who got hurt on the fast rope and another guy just got hit. He may not have survived.' I was pretty sure he hadn't, but then, I didn't know for sure.

Soon after, we whipped through the gate into the airport compound, where a scene of frenzy confronted us. Guys were running everywhere, loading helicopters, loading vehicles, and scrambling for more ammo. The medical team was waiting as I had requested. They began pulling Pilla out of the back of my Humvee. When I saw his face, as white as a snow bank, I didn't have to wonder anymore.

'Just leave him alone,' I said to Doc Marsh. 'He's gone. Go to the other vehicle. Blackburn's over there.' Medics began racing in that direction.

The Hard Part

Now there was nothing further for me to do. I walked away from my vehicle as a wave of fury swept over me. It had been the worst, most intense 40 minutes of my life. What a stupid situation. The mission had been going so well – until this. We had lost one of the best guys ever to wear the Ranger scroll on his uniform and another one was in serious jeopardy. This whole thing was disgusting.

I realised my squad were waiting for me to speak. I searched for words to explain all the bullets and blood we'd just been through. I tried to think of how I could smooth over the hurt they were feeling but I couldn't come up with anything, so I kept my mouth shut.

Just then, the air was changed by the approach of Lieutenant

Larry Moores, the officer in charge of my platoon. A man well into his thirties, he was older than most lieutenants and was known to be a meticulous planner, yet he trusted us subordinates greatly, having been in our shoes as an enlisted man before he was commissioned. His face now was drained; I knew immediately that something was very wrong.

'What's up, sir?' I asked.

Very slowly he answered, 'Another Black Hawk has gone down. You need to get your squad ready to go back in. We need to get to the crash site.'

'What do you mean, *another?*' I cried. 'We're losing birds now?'

'Yes. Wolcott's went down while you were out and now we just found out that Mike Durant's is down as well.'

I was dumbfounded. After all the disaster we'd just come through, we were being told to head right back into it again?

Acknowledging the fact that a Ranger is a more elite soldier who arrives at the cutting edge of battle by land, sea, or air... is what our Creed said. 'Readily will I display the intestinal fortitude required to fight on to the Ranger objective and complete the mission...' Now was the time to prove it.

'Sergeant Mitchell!' I called to my team leader. 'Get your vehicle down to the supply point and get more ammo! Get some for us, too, while you're at it. And don't forget to fuel up.

Death Up Close

As we prepared the vehicle to go back out, the radio in front kept transmitting the sounds of the worsening battle in the city. Dozens of voices, it seemed, were talking on top of each other and what struck me was not only the fact of guys getting pinned down and shot at but, even more, the rising urgency in their tone. Everybody sounded as though he were yelling at somebody a thousand miles away. Calls for MEDEVACs, pleas for reinforcement − you could sense the wave of fear starting to sweep across the battlefield. The situation was growing worse by the minute.

I hung on every word. With each new voice, I pictured in my mind the face of the speaker. It was becoming clear that we were not battling just a thousand or so militia fighters in the streets of

Mogadishu; we could have handled that many. This was sounding more like ten thousand. There seemed to be no end to their resources.

Occasionally my heart would soar as a commander gave confident direction to his soldiers on the radio. Then just as quickly, my spirit would sink as another frazzled sergeant would say, 'We're getting clobbered here; we really need some help.' I knew the sensation all too well.

Finally I said to Kerr, 'Turn the radio off. I don't even want to hear what's happening for a while.' We didn't have time to be distracted; we needed to get ready to move out again.

The relative silence allowed new thoughts to surface in my mind: 'I'm going to die tonight. And what's just as bad, I'm going to get every one of my men killed. I just know it. There's no way we can survive another run back into that city. Tomorrow, this squad is going to have ten dead Rangers instead of just one.'

My mind then wandered to my wife, Dawn, newly pregnant. 'My child is never going to know his daddy,' I thought. 'This is it, tonight. How is she going to manage having a baby and raising it all by herself?' I started to pray. It was a very simple prayer. 'God, I'm in deep trouble, as you can see. I need help. I'm not saying you should get me out of this. I just need your help.'

Still scrubbing away at the blood in the back of the wagon, my attention veered off somehow to an ancient scene: the Lord Jesus praying in the Garden of Gethsemane. I was no longer in Somalia at that moment. I was echoing the prayer of Jesus, 'My Father, if it is possible, let this cup pass from Me; yet not as I will, but as You will.'[2]

My life was in God's hands, I told myself, and the only thing I could do at this critical point was to trust Him with the course of events. The hour and circumstances of my death were up to Him. I could definitely die tonight. Of course, I could get killed crossing the street back in America, too. I could slip on a bar of soap in the shower and hit my head.

If I survived this night, I would get to go home eventually to Dawn and our new baby. If I died, I'd go home to be with the Lord Jesus in heaven. Either way, I'd be a winner. So maybe I needed to stop being afraid of the upcoming battle after all.

A second realisation then came my way. I had a leadership role to fulfil. 'God, please don't let me do anything stupid that puts the rest of my men at risk of slaughter tonight,' I prayed. 'If any of them gets killed, I sure don't want it to be my fault.'

Suddenly a surreal sense of peace came over me: it was the peace the Bible describes as ' comprehension, [which] will guard your hearts and your minds in Christ Jesus.'[3] I snapped back out of my reverie, took a visual inspection of the vehicle, and said, 'Men, we're good. Let's load up and get ready to move.' We returned to the rest of the squad, where Danny Mitchell had the preparations in good order.

One of my slightly older men, Brad Thomas, was definitely struggling, I could tell. He had married just a few months before coming here. Now I was asking him to head straight back into the teeth of destruction. He pulled me aside to say, 'Sergeant, you know, I *really* don't want to go back out.'

This was a costly thing for a Ranger to say. He knew there would be consequences for shrinking from the fight. He had apparently weighed that price and decided to pay it.

Now what was I, his sergeant, going to do? I reviewed the options in my mind. I could end his career in the Ranger Regiment right here by saying 'Go back to your cot and pack up your stuff – you're on the next plane out of here!'

I opted instead for a more nuanced approach. 'Listen, I understand how you feel,' I said in a low tone. 'I'm married too. Don't think of yourself as a coward. I know you're scared. I have never been in a situation quite like this, either.

But we've got to go. It's our job. The difference between being a coward and a hero is not whether you're scared or not. It's what you do *while* you're scared.'

I don't know to this day where I got that line. It was nothing I had read in a book or heard from a speaker. I guess God just gave it to me when I needed it. I turned my attention back to the demands of the moment.

Brad Thomas walked away for a moment, thinking hard. I climbed into my Humvee and, in a minute, glanced at the rear view mirror. There I saw Brad climbing aboard with the rest of us. We were ready to roll in search of that downed Black Hawk that needed us.

* * *

One of my last memories of Somalia was sitting on a canvas and metal bunk in the bombed-out aeroplane hangar on the Mogadishu airfield once the mission had been completed. Many Rangers and men from some of the other units with me in Somalia were coming up to me asking questions about faith and about Jesus Christ. Often they were worried about dying. It struck me how similar their questions were to the ones I asked as a child dealing with my own death. I had many conversations about faith and about how Jesus Christ conquered sin by His death on the cross and how He conquered death and the grave by His resurrection. It was during some of those conversations under the hot African sun that I felt God indicate that He wanted me to help warriors deal with eternal matters. It was in Somalia that God changed my life from battle-hardened warrior to minister of the Gospel of Jesus Christ.

3

James Gardiner

Man of Courage and Conviction

By Faith Cook

The Battle of Ramillies raged fiercely. Massed French troops were pitted against the combined forces of the English, Austrian, and Dutch armies, a coalition called *The Grand Alliance*. Hostilities had begun in 1701 when Louis XIV of France attempted to claim the disputed succession to the Spanish throne for the French crown. It became immediately obvious that if France and Spain were to unite under French domination, England would be in grave danger. Led by the charismatic Duke of Marlborough, John Churchill, the tide was beginning to turn against Louis, first at the Battle of Blenheim in 1704 and now in 1706 at this decisive encounter near the Belgian village of Ramillies not far from Maastricht.

Casualties on both sides were heavy and lying among the 3,000 or more dead and wounded of Marlborough's men was eighteen-year-old James Gardiner. Courageous and fearless, James was a Scottish boy born into a family with strong military traditions. Despite a religious upbringing, James had no time or thought for God and his only ambition was to achieve glory on the battlefield. Deputed to clear a stubborn rump of the French military from a graveyard in Ramillies, James had the misfortune to be shot in the mouth by the enemy. With a cry, he fell to the ground as the battle continued to roar around him. In normal circumstances such a wound would have killed him outright but, surprisingly, James remained conscious.

As the noise of battle gradually faded into the distance, he gingerly felt around his mouth. Yes, his teeth were still intact – so was his tongue. What had happened? Perhaps he had swallowed the bullet? Then he realised he was bleeding from the back of his neck. Amazingly, the shot had passed right through his mouth without any major damage and emerged at the back of his neck. However, blood was steadily seeping from the wound.

Would no one help him? As he lay alone on that May evening, he knew without help he must soon bleed to death. Night fell, the temperature dropped, and still no one came. James Gardiner was left among the dead and dying, alone with his thoughts and his pain. His chief anxiety, however, was not his eternal destiny if he died before morning, but a small cache of gold he carried in his pocket. If God was to spare his life, he reasoned, he would need that gold. With slow, painful movements he grasped the coins and sealed them in his clenched fist with his own congealed blood.

As the first streaks of dawn stole across the sky, looters streamed out of the village, stealing anything of value from the dead and killing any who still showed signs of life. James was aware of a raised sword above him. This was the end. Then he heard a voice saying, 'Do not kill that poor child.'[4] The looter turned to his next victim. Struggling to open his eyes, James looked into a kindly face – a local friar. Unable to speak, he indicated his desperate need of a drink. From a small vial the friar carried he poured a few drops of brandy down the young soldier's throat.

As a little strength returned, James Gardiner managed to gasp in a hoarse whisper that he wished to be carried to the nearby village of Huy, where, so he said, he had relatives. Believing the story to be true, the compassionate friar made arrangements for the wounded man to be put on a barrow and wheeled to the place he had indicated. Each jolt along the uneven path sent a searing arrow of pain through the wounded man's whole body. Surely they must reach Huy soon? However, gradually the dreadful truth dawned. They were lost: they had followed the wrong track through a thick wood.

James could bear no more. To think of a further night of agony was too much. He begged the men who carried him either to kill him outright or else leave him alone to die in the woods. Faced with such a dilemma the men decided to wheel Gardiner to a nearby convent. At least he would be treated with kindness and perhaps die with a modicum of comfort.

The nuns received James sympathetically and dressed his wound. Later the local barber-surgeon arrived and did a little primitive surgery on it. Surprisingly, James, a tough and physically strong young man, began to recover and to the astonishment of all regained his health in three months.

Anxious to convert him to the Roman Catholic faith, the nuns repeatedly urged his need of gratitude to God and to the Virgin Mary for his deliverance from death. But, grateful as he was for their kindness, James had no interest in their admonitions. All he

wanted was to return to the battlefield, and with an exchange of
prisoners he found himself back on home ground. Honoured for his
courage in the Battle of Ramillies, the young man was soon raised
to the rank of Lieutenant.

An Earthly Crown

Back in the forefront of many a fray, James Gardiner found himself
quickly promoted and he was awarded a commission in the
regiment of the Scots Greys. Narrowly escaping further wounds,
Gardiner proved himself both fearless and skilled. Further honours
and advancements followed in quick succession until he received
a commission as Captain-Lieutenant[5] of a regiment of the King's
Dragoons with a personal acknowledgement of his services from
King George I himself.

Only two things mattered to James Gardiner: his prowess on
the battlefield and the more clandestine conquests he could make
of any attractive woman he met in his leisure hours. He cared little
about the God of whom his widowed mother had faithfully taught
him, feeling nothing more than self-congratulation for his many
deliverances in battle. Night after night the young officer could be
found flirting with any woman foolish enough to be lured by his
handsome appearance and winsome personality.

In 1715, James Gardiner, now 27, was serving in France under
the Earl of Stair, one of England's foremost military commanders of
the time. Despite his dissolute lifestyle, Gardiner kept both eyes and
ears open for any plans the French, now supposedly at peace with
England, might be hatching. None other than James Stuart, son of
James II, who had been ousted from the English throne in 1688, was
living at the French court under the protection of Louis XIV. James
Stuart wanted to see his family re-established on the English throne.
With the unpopular Hanoverian George I recently crowned King of
England, it seemed the right moment to strike.

Gardiner caught wind of the impending invasion, planned to
take place in a mere six weeks' time. He informed the Earl of Stair,
who despatched him post-haste to London to raise the alarm, so
giving the military time to prepare its defences. Soon news trickled
through that French troops had actually landed in Scotland and
were aiming to make common cause with secret Stuart supporters

in both Scotland and England. James Gardiner rode hastily north with a small band of men. By the time he reached Preston, not far from Blackpool, James Stuart's French troops, together with his enthusiastic Scottish Highlanders, were streaming south, having already won some significant victories. Now they aimed to press on to London, hoping to gather further English allies as they went.

However, they had reckoned without James Gardiner and his dedicated men. Fearlessly he led his unit forward, dashing into a hail of enemy fire, before setting fire to a barricade the enemy had erected. Astonished by the ferocity of the assault, the Stuart forward troops, many of them untrained in warfare, hastily fell back, contributing to a general retreat of the invading army. Many of Gardiner's men also fell that day, but once again their brave Captain escaped without injury. Further accolades followed for James Gardiner when it became clear that the first Jacobite rebellion was effectively over. Preston had marked the most southern point the invading forces would reach.

Despite all his achievements and all his admirers, Gardiner was not a happy man. Carefree and casual outwardly, he struggled inwardly to reconcile his dissolute and dishonourable personal life with those standards and truths he knew to be right. At no point did he become a sceptic: he realised well that one day he would have to answer before God for his immoral conduct. Added to this, Gardiner was honest enough to know that any prayers he offered were unacceptable to God while he continued in his present way of life. Not wishing to be guilty of hypocrisy, he decided to give up all attempts at prayer or any other religious observances. On one occasion a fellow officer congratulated him on a particularly unsavoury conquest he had recently made of some naïve woman. Just at that moment a dog entered the room. 'I wish I were that dog,' thought the unhappy man. At least the dog would not have to face any final judgement.

A Surprise Encounter

Gardiner, now a Major, was back in Paris following the defeat of the first Jacobite rebellion. It was a Sunday evening in July 1719, a date he would never forget. With all his day's duties completed, he attended a social function that ended at about 11 o'clock, but his day was not finished, for at midnight he had an assignation – a secret rendezvous with a married woman. With an hour to kill he returned to his quarters and paced restlessly around his room as the minutes crept by. Bored, he picked up a book, blew off the dust, and began to turn the pages. The title had arrested his attention: *The Christian Soldier,* written by one Thomas Brooks, a Puritan theologian of an earlier generation.

Carelessly Gardiner flipped over the pages. With a candle as his only light it was not easy to read the print, but suddenly a blaze of light flooded across his page. He glanced up in surprise. Had the flare come from the candle guttering? No, it was burning as steadily as before. He raised his eyes higher and what he saw astonished and frightened the proud Major, riveting him to the spot.

Shining above him, he saw a representation of the Lord Jesus Christ dying on the cross. Radiating outwards, bright rays of light filled the room, penetrating the darkest corners. Dumbstruck, Gardiner gazed at the vision, transfixed and amazed. Then he heard a voice – or was it a voice? Afterwards he was not quite sure. Perhaps the words were scorched into his mind so clearly that he only thought he had actually heard them, but later, on balance, he decided it was the former. 'O sinner!' he heard, 'Did I suffer this for you, and are these your returns?' Gardiner had no answer. Gradually the bright vision faded.

How long he sat there, scarcely able to move, he never knew. All thoughts of his midnight liaison were forgotten. At last he rose from his seat in a storm of passion and grief and paced back and forth until he was almost fainting with exhaustion and pain. Had he, the popular, successful military man, spent all his life crucifying the Son of God afresh by his sins? Scenes from his past flashed in accusing succession before his eyes: his mother's prayers, the intervention of the friar that had saved his life, the kindness of the nuns, his many escapes from danger, and then his own ugly way of life, the sordid sins that had polluted both mind and body. Only one punishment was his due – hell. He must surely face the just retribution of God for all he had done in despising the crucified Saviour.

Before he left his room the following morning two things seemed clear. The vision was a preliminary warning of his forthcoming death. Shortly he must face the offended Christ to receive the punishment he deserved and, secondly, in the time remaining to him he must do his utmost, however feebly, to make amends and to bring glory to the God whom he had so wronged. He did not expect mercy: he did not even dare to hope for mercy. The thought that there might be pardon for his sins was far from his mind. But something else had also happened to James Gardiner. He had discovered that he had no further desire for those dissolute relationships that had so long disgraced his life and in their place came a deep longing for secret and personal prayer and for listening to preaching from the Bible.

Overwhelming Glory

For three months Gardiner remained in this state of remorse and foreboding. Why had death not already come? Could it be possible that God would show him mercy after all? Gradually a small flicker of hope kindled in his mind. At last, in October 1719, he heard a sermon based on the Epistle to the Romans that declared to the broken man a full 'remission for sins that are past,'[6] and the gift of Christ's righteousness in place of his own unrighteousness.

The flicker of hope burst into a flame of joy. Gardiner was ecstatic with relief and gratitude to a God of mercy and grace. For three nights he could scarcely sleep for, as he afterwards expressed it, 'Glory seemed to overwhelm my soul.' The first to be told of this remarkable change was his mother, a faithful woman whose prayers and tears had long followed her son. Nor could his associates fail to notice the change in James Gardiner. The Major has gone 'stark mad,' reported some.

Never one to duck a challenge, Gardiner decided that he would seek an opportunity to explain to these bemused and sceptical men what had happened to him. Soon afterwards he and his fellow officers were invited to spend a few days at the country home of a member of the nobility. Gardiner asked his host if he could arrange an evening dinner when all his fellow officers were present and then allow him to address the company.

Somewhat mystified, his host agreed. Asking for a tolerant hearing, James Gardiner plunged into a defence and an explanation of the astonishing changes they had seen in him. Open-mouthed, they listened. And, before anyone could mock, he challenged them to demonstrate how a corrupt and irreligious lifestyle could possibly be better than one of contentment and peace. The fear of sudden and violent death was always lurking not far from the surface in the minds of these military men, so now Gardiner challenged them to compare their fears with the solid certainty of a life of glory awaiting the believer beyond the grave. His fellow officers were totally silenced. Eventually the host summed up the response of many: 'We thought this man mad, but he is in good earnest proving that we are so.'

A Profound Change and Marriage

Clearly a profound change had taken place in James Gardiner. And the change filtered through to every part of his life. In days when the army was billeted in the homes of the residents in the various towns and villages to which they were sent, the locals would dread the arrival of the military. Hospitality might be abused: frequently the soldiers would plunder and steal from their hosts, even dishonouring their wives and girls. Things quickly changed wherever Gardiner's units were billeted. Discipline was tightened and swearing and blasphemy forbidden, with swift but just penalties for offenders.

Fair and kind to the men under his command, Gardiner often chose to be quartered in the same conditions as they. On one occasion, however, he decided on a midnight walk. To his surprise, he discovered one man supposed to be on sentry duty who had abandoned his post, a serious fault. When the offender felt a firm grip on his arm he responded with a stream of oaths, only to be silenced when he realised to whom he was speaking. Appropriate punishment followed, accompanied by a stern reprimand. But the man knew well he had escaped lightly. In addition to firm discipline in the regiment there was clear evidence that Gardiner cared personally for his men. If anyone was sick he ensured that the sick man received the best care available and visited his quarters each day, almost as a father would watch over his children. In response his soldiers loved him and performed their duties with an eye to pleasing him.

Many could only wonder at the changes in Gardiner, having known him in former days. To just a select few did he confide the details of that extraordinary night that had so altered his conduct and lifestyle, but it was generally known that no day passed without the Colonel leaving his bed at five each morning to spend the first hour of the day in secret prayer. Sometimes an emergency required that he order his unit to make a forced march, beginning at first light of dawn. Even this did not deter Gardiner, who rose even earlier than usual to pray.

Not until 1726, at the age of 38, did James Gardiner marry. Lady Frances Erskine came from a distinguished Scottish family and proved an ideal wife for an army officer. Unselfish and gentle, she did not complain that so often James's military duties took him away from home for long periods at a time. Sometimes this involved lengthy campaigns on the Continent or in the north of England. The only compensation for her loneliness was the detailed and loving letters James wrote to her. Her one fault, as he jovially remarked, was that 'she valued and loved him more than he deserved.'

On Lady Frances fell the responsibility of caring on her own for their numerous family, for thirteen infants were born to the couple in quick succession. On her too fell the burden of their many bereavements, for eight of the children died in infancy or early childhood. In one instance, James had just posted a letter to his wife to tell her of his relief and joy on hearing that a young son was recovering from smallpox, a scourge that took so many children to an early grave. Then came grievous news that the child had just died. However, the loss that almost broke the Colonel and his wife was that of their second son, an unusual and promising six-year-old. Loved by all for his sunny disposition and his bright, intelligent remarks, the boy's death, after an illness of only fifteen hours, was a stroke hard to bear. How would the family cope with such grief, his friends wondered? It was hard indeed. James and Frances could only look to God for His help in their dire need and trust His hidden but wise purposes. These things made them both think often of the joys of heaven that could not be snatched away by death.

Not long after his conversion, Gardiner had a strange and vivid dream. He was walking across a field – a field he knew well, for it was near the place of his birth. It led to the gate of the small church in Tranent with its surrounding graveyard. Ahead of him walked a figure. Who could it be? Suddenly, in his dream he recognised the figure as none other than Christ Himself, but why did He not turn round and walk with the Colonel or even give him a welcoming smile? Perplexed, Gardiner kept on following the figure until they reached the gate of the church. Here at last Christ (for Gardiner was convinced that it was He) turned around and gave him a radiant smile. What could this mean, Gardiner asked himself on waking?

At last he decided that the only interpretation was that sometimes Christ calls his people to follow Him without any apparent sign of His approval or encouragement, but at the hour of death, Gardiner felt assured, Christ would turn and smile on him. It was a dream he never forgot.

An Emerging Threat

New wars had broken out on the Continent in 1739, this time over the succession to the Austrian throne following the death of their king, Charles VI. Jealous eyes were all on that throne, for the only obvious successor was a woman, Charles's daughter, Maria Theresa, and a clause in the country's constitution stipulated that no woman could inherit the crown. Britain and the Dutch Republic thought differently and joined forces with the Austrian army to help them fight for their rightful queen. No Englishman man could forget the successful reign of their own Queen Elizabeth but their motives were not entirely altruistic, for the French, Spanish, and Italians who joined forces against Austria were hoping to increase their domination on the Continent, a situation England feared. Colonel Gardiner and much of the English army were therefore frequently abroad during these years. But during 1744 and into 1745 he and his regiment had returned to England.

Peaceful years they were on the home front – perhaps a little too peaceful, for under the benign Prime Minister, Robert Walpole, · whose motto was 'let sleeping dogs lie,' the country was off its guard. Secret plots were still being hatched in the French court, this time to put Charles Stuart, known as *Bonnie Prince Charlie*, on the English throne. An abortive attempt was made in 1744, but intercepted by English battleships. Many English and Scottish sympathisers, particularly in the Tory party, were prepared to fight for the restoration of the Stuarts if circumstances were looking hopeful. A message was sent from a group of such dissidents suggesting that, with the army largely engaged in wars on the Continent, the summer of 1745 might well be the right time to try again.

Borrowing money and purchasing ships, Charles Stuart once again set sail for Scotland, where he knew he had considerable support among the Highlanders. Once again the English intercepted his ships, off the Cornish coast, and many were beaten back. What they did not know was that the ship on which Prince Charles himself was sailing had escaped the fray and on 23 July Charles landed on the Island of Eriskay in the Outer Hebrides. A few days later he crossed to the mainland, unknown to the English. Rumours began to seep through of a forthcoming Jacobite uprising, but George II and the army generals largely discounted them as hearsay. The prevailing wisdom was that, as a Dutch contingent was soon expected on English soil, it would be on hand to defend the English throne if any problems should arise.

Before long, enthusiastic Highland chiefs gathered their clans in support of Charles Stuart and began swooping down from their upland fortresses in hordes. Alarm bells started to sound in the court of George II when it was rumoured that first Perth and then Coatbridge had fallen to surprise attacks and Jacobite rebels were advancing steadily towards Edinburgh. Sir John Cope was Commander-in-Chief of the Scottish army. Though frequently successful in his Continental campaigns, he seemed strangely lethargic over this Jacobite rebellion. Eventually he sent a small and largely untrained detachment south from his Inverness base, with the infantry marching to a rallying point south of Dunbar and the cavalry sailing down the coast. The Highlanders meanwhile swept on their victorious way armed with anything they could lay hands on: pikes, pitchforks, and scythes as well as an assortment of other armaments.

In early September Colonel James Gardiner and his 13th Regiment marched hastily up the country. Gardiner, now 57, had often pondered on heaven and the life to come, its reality ever present both because of his occupation and of the sorrows of his family life. 'Oh eternity, eternity!' he had once exclaimed to his friend Philip Doddridge, well-known Dissenting pastor and hymn-writer, 'What a wonderful thought is eternity! All complaints shall be for ever banished and nothing separate between God and our souls.' Perhaps such thoughts were now filling his mind. He must have been glad to know that his much-loved wife, Lady Frances, and his eldest daughter were presently staying in Stirling and so would not be far away.

By mid-September the alarming news came that Edinburgh itself had fallen to the Jacobite troops of Charles Stuart. Cheering crowds encouraged the *Young Pretender*, as he was known, on his triumphant way and soon his father, James Stuart, who had tried unsuccessfully to capture the English throne in 1715, was crowned James VIII of Scotland with Charles, his son, serving as his regent. The situation was dire.

Fast action was needed if George II's forces were to stand any chance of halting the advance of the Highland troops in their present euphoric mood. James Gardiner knew this well. His long military experience had taught him that surprise attack and decisive action often held the key to victory. As he set out to prepare his regiment of dragoons and infantry for hostilities he said a tender goodbye to Lady Frances and to his daughter. To his surprise Frances suddenly burst into tears and clung to him. 'I fear I will lose you,' she sobbed. Never before had she reacted like this when her husband had set off on some engagement. Kindly and gently, James released himself from her grasp but instead of reassuring her that all would be well he merely said, 'We have eternity to spend together.'

Meeting up with Sir John Cope, Gardiner urged immediate surprise action. The rebels, flushed with their early victories, were in exultant mood and had 4,500 infantry and 400 horse at their command. Sir John and the English army must attack at first light while the enemy was scarcely awake: it was their only hope, Gardiner insisted. However, to his utter dismay, Sir John seemed in no hurry to take action, preferring to answer the enemy's first moves with his counter-strategy. Recognising that this undoubtedly spelt defeat, Gardiner could only reply, 'I have one life to sacrifice for my country's safety and I will not spare it.'

Prepared as he was to sacrifice his all, he was not equally sure of his men's commitment. Some were raw recruits who had never seen action, while others were untried in the face of overwhelming odds. As daylight faded on the night of 19th September 1745, Gardiner lined up his troops in battle formation just outside Prestonpans, a few miles east of Edinburgh and not far from the village of Tranent. Riding in and out among his men before they relaxed for the night, he urged them to stand firm whatever the cost. He could do no more. Their cause was right and good, he declared, and the prosperity of the Protestant church would be under severe threat if the Stuarts regained the throne. The memory of the 'killing times' under Charles Stuart's grandfather James II, who had brutally crushed Protestant dissenting voices in favour of the Roman Catholic Church, could not be forgotten. Later that evening Gardiner was seen walking alone, lost in thought.

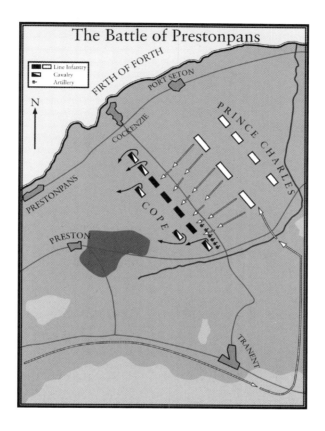

Faithful unto Death

The night was long and tense. Colonel Gardiner spent it astride his horse, sheltering in the protection of a haystack. At about three in the morning he called his four bodyguards, whose responsibility it was to care for him. Three of them he discharged affectionately from their duties, urging them to care for their own safety but above all for their eternal destiny. The fourth, John Foster, one who had served him long and loyally, was to remain with him. In all probability James spent the next hour in private prayer and mental preparation for the battle ahead. The situation was fraught with danger, as he well knew.

Scarcely had the first light of dawn streaked across the Scottish sky when a ghastly cry broke the silence, followed by sickening yells and furious volleys of gunfire. The enemy had struck. Rebel troops

swarmed across the large open field that lay between the two camps,
brandishing their weapons, slashing their scythes to right and left,
and cutting down any man or horse who charged forward to meet
them. Gardiner and his men dashed into battle to check the advance
but almost immediately Gardiner received a wound in the chest.
His dragoons, who made up his left wing, wavered, broke ranks,
and fled. Despite the searing pain Gardiner fought on, though now
dangerously exposed on his left flank. Suddenly, another shot hit
him on his right thigh. Desperately, he tried to rally the remnant of
his dragoons but soon discovered that all but a handful had turned
tail and retreated from the onslaught.

John Foster, his faithful bodyguard and attendant, remained at
his side but begged his master to retreat before he received a fatal
wound. Just as Gardiner was considering such an option, he noticed
a small group of leaderless infantry men fighting valiantly nearby.
'Those brave fellows will be cut in pieces for want of a commander,'
he yelled. Spurring on his horse he rode to their head. 'Fire on, my
lads, and fear nothing,' he called out encouragingly.

No sooner had he spoken those words than a Highlander rode
menacingly towards him brandishing a scythe tied to the end of a
long pole. He rushed at Gardiner and with one aggressive swipe
deeply wounded him in his right arm. Gardiner's sword dropped
and the brave Colonel fell from his horse. 'Take care of yourself,'
he shouted to Foster, who was still at his side. Another Highlander,
recognising that the man on the ground was a valued prize, struck
him a final desperate blow on the head. The last words Gardiner
was heard to articulate before he lost consciousness are said to
have been, 'You are fighting for an earthly crown. I go to receive a
heavenly one.'

The battle was over in five short minutes. The excited Highlanders
raced on their victorious way. King George II's troops had been
routed in what was perhaps the shortest battle in the annals of the
times. Foster ran for his life to a nearby mill. He exchanged his
uniform for a disguise as a miller's servant and, taking horse and
cart, returned to the battlefield. The last service he could do for his
honoured master was to retrieve his body from among the dead. All
was quiet: the roar of battle had been exchanged for an eerie silence.
Foster quickly found Gardiner. To his astonishment, he discovered
that the Colonel was still alive. His watch and boots had already
been stolen by plunderers. His horse too had gone, to be ridden, so

it is said, by Charles himself on his march south as he penetrated as far as Derby, an advance that was to mark the furthest point of his triumphant foray.

Gently lifting his dying master, Foster laid him as carefully as he could in the cart and set off across the field to the little church of Tranent, the very church of Gardiner's dreams. From here the dying man was taken to the minister's house, but by eleven o'clock that morning the trumpeters of heaven sounded a clarion call of victory for Colonel Gardiner as he passed beyond the pain and noise of battle – faithful until death.

The Death of Colonel James Gardiner (1688-1745) at the Battle of Prestonpans in 1745.

4

Doc Watt

A God-Driven Man of Steel and Compassion

*Surgeon Vice Admiral Sir James Watt KBE, CSTJ, MD, MS, FRCP,
FRCS, FSA (1914–2009)*

By Richard Blake

Many sailors felt ill that day in February 1943 when savage weather roused the North Atlantic to a frenzied storm, but a young Royal Naval Volunteer Reserve (RNVR) Surgeon Lieutenant was fighting a kidney infection as well. During the middle watch he would ordinarily have been on bridge duty with the First Lieutenant but this night he was confined to his bunk. The wind shrieked and moaned, raising massive green seas with menacing wave-crests that streamed with foam. Ships rolled dangerously or butted into walls of water that had the power to smash metalwork and tear away everything unsecured. This was ship-killing weather. HMS *Roxborough* was an obsolescent, four-funnelled destroyer, American built, designed for the Pacific, and transferred to the British navy under Lend-Lease. She rolled badly at the best of times and under these dangerous conditions she was heading into the storm as she struggled to make it back to Newfoundland from her patrol line off Greenland, having escorted a British-bound convoy from North America to mid-Atlantic, where other escorts took over. During the hours of darkness a sister destroyer was overwhelmed by the sea and foundered without trace.

Suddenly, the *Roxborough* was struck by a huge green sea that pulverised and tore away most of the bridge structure, killing the Captain in the wreckage of his sea cabin, causing horrific injury to the First Lieutenant, and sweeping away the lives of another nine men. The ship was in mortal danger, lacking rudder control from the smashed wheelhouse, and faced the risk of falling into the trough of the waves, broadside-on to seas that would engulf and sink her. The senior surviving seaman officer was a Canadian Sub-Lieutenant, now charged with the urgent responsibility of getting the vessel under steerage-way[7] using hand apparatus and attempting some kind of damage control. The skill of the deck department in conning the stricken ship back to St John's harbour in Newfoundland was a minor epic of seamanship.

HMS ROXBOROUGH (formerly USS FOOTE) moored.

Meanwhile, there was urgent life-saving work for the surgeon. He was James Watt, known universally as *Doc Watt* and as a staunch – even outspoken – Christian. These mind-numbing and frightening circumstances were the crucible of fire in which faith's reality would be tested both for him and for those who were watching. He could not let his own state of health form part of the calculation. He and a pair of Able Seamen went round the ship searching for casualties. They extracted a desperately injured First Lieutenant from the torn and mangled wreckage that had once formed the bridge structure. Several others had been badly smashed by the impact of the freak wave and they needed urgent medical attention. As the ship bucked around in the storm the casualties were identified and brought to the stokers' mess aft, well-nigh the only dry compartment remaining, and now turned into an emergency makeshift surgery. Watt prepared as best he could as the ship twisted and pitched in wild seas, with his surgical instruments in a mess-tin nailed down to a wooden table. On each side was a sailor securely lashed to an upright stanchion to keep them steady while they in turn kept a firm hold on the surgeon as he tried to perform delicate, life-saving surgical procedures.

The first patient was the First Lieutenant, who had lost a leg and had suffered other catastrophic injuries. Only the night before, Doc Watt had been speaking to him about the Christian faith but without apparent success: no, he reckoned he was all right as he was and thought he could pray to God whenever it suited him. Now the surgeon prepared to operate, beginning procedures with a prayer of his own, but to his dismay his patient died in front of him before Watt could do anything to save his life. Now seriously shaken and unwell, Watt took a few minutes to get to his cabin and recover himself. And when he reached it he found that God had gone before him.

The cabin was in confusion after the impact of the sea and his books had been pitched out onto his bunk. His Bible was there amongst them, lying open at the account of Paul's experience of a protracted storm in the Mediterranean that ended with shipwreck on the coast of Malta. A particular verse caught Doc's eye: 'Do not be afraid, Paul… God has granted you all those who are sailing with you.'[8] What an assurance of hope for a battered servant of God! It gave him fresh strength and confidence, rekindling faith and calming fear. To Doc it was better than 'splicing the mainbrace,' for he took these words as a promise from the living, present, gracious

Lord of Life. It gave him the inner resources he needed to perform his medical task and to fulfil his further responsibilities as the senior officer left on board.

Back to the improvised surgery he went, back to his trusty supporters and the damaged men who relied on his skill and compassion. Over the next two days he scarcely had time to rest as he operated on eighteen casualties and God fulfilled the promise of Scripture, for each one recovered from his injuries. When the *Roxborough* berthed at St John's it seemed entirely appropriate that her company should muster on the upper deck for a church service taken by a Chaplain, supported by Doc Watt, to give thanks to God for their deliverance from the great storm (perhaps the worst of the war) and to remember before Him the colleagues who had not survived.

Though he did not know it yet, the grateful and grieving Surgeon Lieutenant RNVR was on his way to becoming a future Medical Director General for the Royal Navy, founder of the Naval Christian Fellowship, and a man whose talent for surgery, administration, and historical scholarship would be recognised internationally.

Going where God Directs

The foundation of Watt's character and career was his faith in Christ as Saviour and Lord. Born in 1914, his formative years were spent in the shadow of the Great War and the period of hope, economic depression, and the menacing shadows of Nazism that followed. His academic abilities, honed at King Edward VI School, Morpeth, suggested a legal career, but his mother's influence helped guide him towards medicine. Accordingly he embarked on a six-year course at Durham University to qualify as a doctor. In 1938, his final year as an undergraduate, Watt accompanied his mother to a church service where he heard a message that changed his life. The preacher clearly had a personal knowledge of God that the medical student lacked and felt he needed. The way to obtain it, Watt thought, was to offer himself as a candidate for baptism. When the time for the service came Watt discovered that he was expected to make a public statement of his faith. Instead, he had to confess that he did not yet have what he was craving, a personal relationship with Christ, and so his baptism became just such a commitment of himself to the Lord as his own

Master and Saviour, the Lamb of God who takes away the sins of the world and makes the believer right with God. Assurance and peace followed as did the conviction that never faltered, that the service of Christ the Lord is the overriding obligation for all who are saved by grace. From that time on Watt was a God-driven man.

In the last months of peace and the early days of war he completed his training as a surgeon and widened his experience in Princess Mary Maternity Hospital, Newcastle upon Tyne. He had already volunteered for the navy but his call-up was delayed until 1941, when he was appointed Surgeon Lieutenant in the fast light cruiser *Emerald*, based at Singapore. Getting to her involved passage in a troop ship and experience of torpedo attack, then a spell in Madras where he had the opportunity of meeting the well-known missionary-doctor Amy Carmichael at Dohnavur. Finally, he reached the *Emerald* as ordered. Soon he was engaged in a full-scale medical emergency, treating badly injured men after a collision with another light cruiser. A different kind of challenge was presented when malaria broke out and fatalities resulted. Then came the devastating success of Japanese arms: the attack on the US fleet at Pearl Harbour, the sinking of HMSs *Prince of Wales* and *Repulse*, the overrunning of the Malayan peninsula, and the onslaught against Singapore. With the fall of the bastion of British power in the Far East imminent, the *Emerald* was detailed to pick up the naval Commander-in-Chief and make her escape to Colombo. Thereafter, she was part of the naval force charged with the protection of Ceylon (as Sri Lanka was called in those days of British rule): the imminence of danger was underlined when the carrier *Hermes* was sunk by air attack the day after the *Emerald* relinquished escort duties and two heavy cruisers were lost the same way.

At this stage, the outcome of the war hung in the balance. The Japanese were supreme in South-East Asia, fighting in the Mediterranean against the Axis forces was not going well, and the Soviet Union was reeling under massive onslaughts from German armour and air power. The Battle of the Atlantic, on which Britain's survival depended, was at its height. Prime Minister Churchill recorded that, nonetheless, he had found a new sense of confidence, for Britain then had allies beyond India, Canada, Australia, and the Empire: not just Stalin's Soviet Union (with his ideas of Marxist-Leninist supremacy) but the USA – democratic, freedom-loving,

English-speaking, with deep roots in Christian values and culture, and with huge industrial potential now committed to defeating Hitler and liberating South-East Asia from the Japanese. It was time for the *Emerald* to be withdrawn to Britain for refit and for her surgeon to be redeployed.

Watt's new ship was the *Roxborough*, escorting convoys from Newfoundland to Greenland, and playing her part in the unrelenting war against the U-boats until storm damage forced her withdrawal. While she was being temporarily patched up in Charleston, Doc was attached to a British-administered shore base in New Jersey where aircrew were being trained. It was known as HMS *Asbury* and had once been a luxury hotel. Here in the USA, far distant from front-line warfare, he and other war-tested men had a welcome opportunity for refreshment. On the other hand, the medical work continued, with casualties of flying accidents to be treated and knowledge to be gained about burns and aviation medicine.

In 1944, as the Allied armies were fighting to liberate Europe, Watt returned to the UK in the *Roxborough* and was appointed to an escort carrier, HMS *Arbiter*. She was American-built and, like all these vessels, had a flight deck and hangar built on a mercantile hull, armed with AA weapons but virtually unarmoured. She had reasonable speed and could carry a modest number of aircraft. Such vessels had been key to winning convoy battles against submarine attack in the North Atlantic, but Arbiter's role was different. In February 1945 she embarked Fleet Air Arm Corsairs of 1843 Squadron and sailed to Sydney, Australia as part of the British Pacific Fleet, where her aircraft were needed as replacements by the fleet carriers. She was not needed in the line of battle, but as soon as the atomic firestorm brought Japan to surrender she acquired a vital humanitarian role, transporting liberated prisoners of war and civilians from Hong Kong to Australia.

As befitted a doctor, and a Christian too, Watt had a deeply compassionate streak in him. More aware than most of what dropping the atom bomb meant in terms of Japanese civilian casualties and of what it might mean for future conflict, he could find no pleasure in the wild and mindless rejoicing of his shipmates at the ending of the Second World War, but he could and did throw himself without reserve into caring for the shaken, emaciated patients now before him, people damaged in body and spirit by what they had suffered, and his efforts earned him a Mention in Despatches.

During the years of war, Doc had experienced the value of Christian fellowship for himself and, in ways not always typical of the British armed forces, he had looked for gatherings where officers and men could share in Bible study and prayer. While the *Emerald* was based at Bombay, he had joined in meetings and activities of the Eastern Fleet Fellowship. While in New Jersey he linked himself with the *Asbury* Fellowship and again in the *Arbiter*, as a Surgeon Lieutenant-Commander, he took the lead in the ship's own Christian fellowship, helping to lead worship in a specially rigged compartment decorated with a large White Ensign. He appreciated how important such gatherings were in strengthening faith under tough conditions, in providing Bible-based teaching, and in attracting people who had never before been willing to consider the claims of Christianity. Might God be calling him to provide much-needed leadership for groups like this? What peacetime plans did God have for his life?

Seeking and Finding the Guidance of God

Back in England, Watt applied to transfer to the Royal Navy but the Admiralty could only offer a one-year engagement with annual extensions thereafter. Disappointed, a now demobilised Doc pursued his medical career in 'Civvy Street' with a spell at Guy's Hospital and a return to Newcastle upon Tyne. He plunged into Christian activity but had no sense that God was blessing it as he had blessed his witness in the Navy. He could not get the Navy out of his mind, not least because of letters he received from naval friends asking him to return to the service. He needed urgently to seek God's mind in this matter before he passed the age when re-enlistment would be allowed.

Out of the blue, a buff envelope with the familiar OHMS title arrived for him. It was from the office of the Navy's Medical Director General, saying that the Admiralty noted he had applied to re-join and enclosing a rail warrant to enable him to attend for interview. It was evidently some kind of administrative error, but when you ask God for guidance can the answer be much clearer than that? The interview took place but there were elements of it that left Doc unsure, particularly when he was told he would have to re-join immediately because of his age. There was still part of his university appointment left to run, but the Navy were prepared to give him until mid-1948 for a final answer. Watt's second term as

The Asbury Fellowship. Doc Watt is pictured on the left of the image.

surgical registrar was due to end on 28th May: was this part of God's perfect timing? Seeking further assurance of God's will, Watt visited the conference centre Hildenborough Hall in Sussex for a weekend break. In the dining room he looked for a vacant place and found himself sitting next to a Leading Sick Berth Attendant from Haslar Naval Hospital. In conversation, the man spoke of difficult times for Christians because of the lack of Godly leadership.

As Watt pondered on these three coincidences – an unexpected Admiralty invitation, an exact match of date when he could be free, and the conversation with a naval medic from the lower deck – he felt the hand of God propelling him. His mind made up, he relinquished his hopes of becoming assistant to the professor of surgery at Durham University and instead re-enlisted in the Royal Navy as a Surgeon Lieutenant at Haslar. He had a career in naval medicine to pursue, of course, but he felt that God had commissioned him to encourage Christian work in the Navy in some special way. He lost no time in developing this new ministry.

Servant Leadership

'Serve to Lead' is the famous motto of the Royal Military Academy Sandhurst, a reminder that leadership is a form of service and that leaders need to learn the art from humble service. Doc Watt exhibited those dual traits of serving and leading. Right from the start at Haslar he linked up with three people: the Hildenborough man, a Christian Wardmaster, Lieutenant Douglas Barnard, and Haslar's Lay Reader, who used to hold small lunchtime gatherings in the chapel vestry. Between them they gathered the names of others to invite, found a suitable room to use, and held the inaugural meeting for a Bible study and prayer group. Twelve people attended, officers and men together, and they resolved to meet regularly in the future. From the start the pattern was established of a weekly gathering to study the Scriptures and a daily lunch-hour meeting to pray: any Christian of whatever service rank or denomination would be welcome. Soon twenty men were regular members.

The work developed, with additional gatherings for prayer and the production of a monthly magazine. At weekends, teams of sailors from Haslar would visit churches in the area to share their testimony to God's faithfulness. At this time, when virtually all able-bodied, eighteen-year-old young men could expect to be called up for a two-year spell in uniform for National Service, there was immediate interest in servicemen everywhere, with all churches and most families feeling some particular sympathy for them. Led by Doc Watt, they were constantly reminded that Christian witness was not just a matter of giving a testimony to people one would probably never meet again, but it was also a daily obligation to live lives of Christian integrity every day in the workplace or home. Members of the Haslar fellowship grew accustomed to praying for one another each morning as they learned the discipline and joy of discipleship.

Then the Admiralty unwittingly played its part in God's plan by directing Watt to Northern Ireland as surgeon at HMS *Gannet*, the RN Air Station at Eglinton. Back at Haslar the move caused dismay, intensified when another senior member was moved to Plymouth and two staunch supporters finished their National Service. Now the lead had to be taken by the younger members, who quickly learned that the only way to face demanding situations is to seek God's guidance and grace through prayer, that often underestimated and under-used resource for all God's people as they acknowledge their complete dependence upon the Holy Spirit's enabling.

With Doc Watt based at HMS *Gannet* from mid-1949 to 1952, the concept of a service-wide fellowship began to develop. The Christian group at the air station found a centre for their own gatherings in a disused hut, converted into a place for meetings for prayer and Bible teaching and a venue for evangelistic films and talks. Members quickly found that they were expected to pray for one another and to witness to their colleagues by words of testimony and lives of consistent Christian conduct. The fellowship grew in numbers and scale of operation: evangelistic meetings to share their faith, weekends away to nourish their faith, and a monthly newsletter to encourage informed prayer. The pattern was replicated in other Naval establishments at Plymouth, Chatham, and Arbroath. In 1950 25 scattered members met at Capernwray Hall in the Lake District for a weekend and decided to form a single association, the *United Naval Christian Fellowship (UNCF)*, with an agreed basis of faith and a monthly periodical to share news for prayer and provide challenging editorials from Watt's pen.

During those post-war years, Britain and the free world believed they faced a global danger from Communism and sheltered behind the collective protection of NATO and the Atlantic Alliance. A high proportion of the national budget went towards defence and, with National Service still obligatory, practically all able-bodied eighteen-year olds could expect a couple of years in uniform. Following an invasion of South Korea by the Communist North, forces were sent to defend it under the auspices of the United Nations. The USA committed massive armaments to the theatre of war and Britain, still very much a world player in those days, sent thousands of men from all three services into a bitter war that lasted from 1950 until 1953. These were the last years of Britain's global empire and various smaller conflicts erupted until colonial rule was replaced by independent governments. The Royal Navy still sent its ships into every ocean of the world and amongst their crews was a fair sprinkling of Christians. As UNCF members found themselves drafted to the Mediterranean, the Persian Gulf, Hong Kong, and the Far East, to ships in home waters and to naval bases around the world, Doc Watt's vision of a prayer-dependent, Gospel-witnessing fellowship spread far beyond Haslar Hospital and Northern Ireland.

Watt began to appreciate why he had been drawn back into the Navy. His idea of a mutually supportive community of believers committed to praying for one another and to sharing their faith with their colleagues was applicable to ships and stations everywhere and his leadership and organisational skill had called something significant into being. He never wanted it to be his own possession and he was happy to draw other people in to share the administrative burden, yet the force of his personality and the dynamism of his faith ensured that the *Naval Christian Fellowship* (as it became) would never be allowed to settle down into casualness, complacency, or compromise.

Faithfulness Rewarded

The services of Surgeon Lieutenant-Commander Watt were required during the Korean War. From July 1952 he was a surgical specialist aboard HM Hospital Ship *Maine* in the Far East, particularly involved with casualties from the conflict. After the *Roxborough* episode and his services in the Pacific theatre at the end of the Second World War, he was already a noted figure in his profession and following this further stretch in Far Eastern waters his reputation became solidly established and he rose rapidly in the Navy. After a spell in the RN Hospital in Hong Kong he was appointed surgical consultant at Plymouth, promoted to Surgeon Commander, and then given successive consultancies at Haslar, in Malta, and back to Haslar. He was known as a Christian, a fine practitioner in his profession, and a capable administrator. The Navy was about to use his talents to the full.

In 1965 Watt became the first Professor of Naval Surgery, again based at Haslar, with particular concern for clinical research and a rise in rank. For four years he held this post, developing various specialist units in naval medicine, until he was promoted to Surgeon Rear Admiral, with a whole new task before him. In 1969 he became the first Dean of Naval Medicine with the awe-inspiring duty of planning and establishing the Institute of Naval Medicine at Alverstoke near Gosport. Long gone were the days when naval and military doctors lagged behind their civilian counterparts, for modern servicemen needed highly sophisticated medical support in the varied and demanding environments in which they were expected to serve and fight.

Doc Watt preaching on HM Hospital Ship Maine.

The Institute rapidly became an internationally recognised centre for research and teaching in matters that affected the health of sailors, particularly aircrew, submariners, and divers. There were environmental health issues of profound significance associated with burns, radiation, the effects of depth pressure on the human physique, and so on. Naval doctors had to devise methods of treatment and preventive regimes. Watt himself was not just an able administrator who re-ordered the career structure for naval consultants, but also a first-rate scientific researcher, with authoritative and innovative treatises on peptic ulcers, burns, and chemotherapy to his credit.

Watt was fascinated by the story behind Haslar Hospital, where so much of his career was conducted. Its origins lay in Commodore

Anson's voyage of 1740 – 44, a brilliant success in many ways but disastrous medically. In the *Centurion* he sailed around the world, surviving hurricane-force storms off Cape Horn, before crossing the Pacific Ocean to carry the war against Spain into Far Eastern waters. The capture of a treasure-laden galleon sailing out of Manila helped his country's finances and provided wealth enough to enrich his crew and to make Anson's fortune. But there was a darker side to the expedition. The *Centurion* should have been accompanied by a small squadron of ships but they were all scattered by storm and loss. Even more appalling was the mortality suffered by the crew as the dread scourge of scurvy exacted the terrible toll of 1,300 dead – compared with four men killed in action. It became evident to Admiralty and parliament that disease was much more dangerous than enemy shot and that protracted maritime operations might be thwarted by ill health. One response was to create at Haslar the finest hospital of the age and to elevate the importance of the Navy's physicians and surgeons by insisting on the highest standards of professional training and pre-entry examination.

Doc Watt relished the task of lifting post-war naval medicine to fresh peaks of excellence in such a setting of historical achievement. He explored the Haslar archives while working at the sharp end of science and technology and he enjoyed the fact that work on nuclear medicine was conducted inside the thick, armoured walls of a *barbette* that once supported the 15-inch gun turret of the last British battleship, HMS *Vanguard*.

In 1972 he reached the peak of his service profession when he became Surgeon Vice Admiral and Medical Director General of the RN. Over the next five years he proved himself a far-sighted administrator, reorganising the career structure and paying particular attention to the way that amphibious operations by the Royal Marines could be given appropriate medical support with surgery speedily available for combat casualties. Five years after his retirement in 1977 these measures were harshly tested in the Falklands War and proved equal to the strain. By the time he left the Navy, Doc Watt had received a knighthood amongst his many medical honours and distinctions. He would have been well-justified in taking his ease amongst his books and paintings to enjoy a relaxed retirement and the plaudits of his profession. On the contrary, a new and fulfilling chapter was about to begin.

Searching for Truth and Wisdom

It would be possible to compile a long list of the societies and associations that competed for a slice of Sir James Watt's time. He was president of the Medical Society of London, which had grown out of an important gathering of naval surgeons in the second half of the eighteenth century to discuss the latest techniques and establish the standards of best practice: by gathering data from whole squadrons of ships they are regarded by some historians as the founding fathers of the science of statistics. He was President of the Royal Society of Medicine and played a major role in redesigning its London headquarters. He continued to write and lecture on many aspects of medicine and public health and was much in demand at national and international conferences.

Careful collection of data had been crucial to his medical researches. That same turn of mind was well fitted to his emergent skills as a historian. In retirement, Sir James made the kind of contribution to naval medical history that could have formed the centrepiece of a distinguished academic career. He wrote with elegance and clarity, making particularly incisive studies of Captains James Cook and George Vancouver, whose voyages of exploration were always limited by the availability of fresh water and appropriate nutrition and affected by the prevalence of water-borne disease. His lectures on Nelson's health, on battle surgery, and on sea-going rations during the Napoleonic War were particularly illuminating. He showed that British survival rates were hugely superior to those of the French because of the Royal Navy's obsession with cleanliness, together with the operation of a crudely effective system of triage, its mastery of surgical techniques, and its custom of making amputations rapidly while the casualty was still dazed and shocked from the effects of a wound. Effective anaesthetics were administered after surgery, as survival rates were found to improve when opiates were given then and not before. After examining the archives in Paris and London, he was able to produce a masterly comparison of contrasting methods of treatment and, though the work was done with impartial concern for the truth, there was no disguising his satisfaction at the conclusion.

Watt largely disposed of the idea that even Tudor surgeons had been barbarously incompetent: he liked to show that they were in line with the best thinking of their own day and with treatments tempered by observation of their patients. The surgeon's chest recovered from the *Mary Rose* supported his view that by then maritime medicine had long outgrown its medieval origins in the trade of the barber-surgeon, better at blood-letting than healing the sick. He drew attention to the excellent work of John Woodall (1570–1643): rational, practical, and humane. In a stream of articles and lectures, Watt explored how a truly scientific profession developed in the eighteenth century with entrance examinations, well-accepted inventories of instruments and drugs, and a forum in which procedures could be reviewed and discussed – a kind of post-graduate school for serving surgeons. As vice-president of the prestigious Society for Nautical Research, visiting professor in the history department of Canada's Calgary University, visiting fellow in the Australian National University, and an internationally acclaimed lecturer, he made a huge contribution to maritime medical history: the Canadian government recognised his work as a member of their archival research team.

It was perhaps his study of the Reverend James Ramsay (1733–89) that brought him most pleasure, for it united medicine, the Navy, and Christian faith. Ramsay had been a highly competent naval surgeon whose career was totally changed by a visit to a slave-trading ship in West Indian waters in 1759. Outraged by what he saw, this man of deep faith and practical piety pledged his life and energies to the overthrow of the Atlantic slave trade and of plantation slavery in the British sugar islands. He became an ordained Anglican clergyman with a parish in the island of St Kitts, where he preached against the iniquities of the system while ministering as best he could to the spiritual and physical well-being of the Negro community. The white planters hated him and tried to evict him from his parish; for eighteen years this heroic and isolated servant of God endured ridicule and opposition as he preached and wrote against slavery, but when he returned to England he had amassed enough documented factual evidence to transform the Abolition movement from a cause of high-minded philosophical principles to an unstoppable parliamentary crusade. Watt crafted a powerful testimony to Ramsay as the 'morning star of the anti-slavery movement' and then wrote him up for the *Oxford Dictionary of National Biography*.

Like Ramsay, Watt was a man of granite-hard principles combined with compassion. His love of truth and his evident integrity made him a much-sought-after speaker and committee member. Well into his nineties he was still producing well-researched material and a final lengthy article on nineteenth-century medical tendencies ashore and afloat was published a few months after his death. The academic world as well as the Navy and the Christian church had all benefited from his energy and intellect.

A Man of God

When Sir James Watt died at the end of 2009, many tributes appeared in the national press and professional journals. Each one noted his Christian faith. For him it was never a clumsy bolt-on to his career but rather the mainspring of his whole character. Ever since those student days when he had become a disciple of the Lord Jesus, his sense of the presence of God and his obligation to serve Him had been overmastering. He knew that nothing half-hearted or slipshod was worthy of the Lord of Heaven and Earth: if he had been called to be a surgeon he must strive to become master of his profession. If administering a complex department with responsibility for a huge budget and a large work-force, he owed it to God and to his colleagues to be efficient and totally trustworthy. He drove himself hard and he expected high standards from those around him. He was no friend to compromise or complacency and this made him disappointed (and even critical) when he encountered such things in churches, hospitals, or politicians. Let truthfulness and integrity drive all public life and let faithfulness to Christ and the Word of God empower the witness of every Christian.

With values like those Watt could never slide into easy-going old age. Like the tree planted by water in the book of Jeremiah, he continued to bear the fruit of God-honouring testimony to the end of his long life. Even when faith is identified as the power that drove him there is still more to say about this remarkable man, for a driving passion such as this can produce a harsh and judgemental character. Instead, it should be clear by now that he was a man of deep compassion. His early training in midwifery and experience of ordinary hospital life after the war gave him insights into the needs of all sorts of people, not just the *macho* community of the Navy. He cherished every appearance of humane values in the historical characters he celebrated. A perfect gentleman of polished courtesy himself, he set standards of gracious behaviour wherever he went. In younger years he had played tennis and rugby with reckless enthusiasm, suffering some quite serious injuries in the process. He remained keen on fitness and mountain walking. He loved music and was a connoisseur of fine paintings. His home was filled with elegant furniture, fine porcelain, pictures, and books. He was an accomplished cook and loved to entertain in style, with the table elegantly laid and flower arrangements that he had made. He was a generous host whose conversation would draw everyone into the circle.

Here was a man who kept company with the best in the land but without a trace of snobbery. In his naval days he had wanted to create a fellowship that transcended ranks and united all Christians in a family of faith. He had no time for pomposity or show. James Watt allowed the Spirit of Christ to shape his character and career, the Lord Christ who did not come to be served but to serve. Such a faith promises salvation for the individual believer: it also transforms people and the community they live in. All are called to live as salt that fights corruption and light that banishes darkness. Doc Watt is an example of what can be achieved by the man or woman who deliberately places themselves in the hand of the Almighty to obey His will.

5

His Name Was Blackadder

By Brigadier WIC Dobbie

His name was Blackadder. My first acquaintance with him occurred as an officer cadet at Sandhurst and this was renewed ten years later when faced with the Staff College examination. At both of these stages of my military education I was required to study the campaigns of one of the most distinguished of all British Army officers, the Duke of Marlborough. The recommended textbook was *Marlborough – His Life and Times*, written by his equally distinguished descendant, Sir Winston Churchill. One of the sources Churchill used in his research was *The Life and Diary of Lieutenant Colonel John Blackadder*. Churchill's quotations from this source reveal that Blackadder was not only a courageous and efficient officer who fought under Marlborough in all four of his greatest battles – Blenheim, Ramillies, Oudenarde, and Malplaquet – but also a simple, devoted, Bible-loving Christian. He clearly won the affection of Winston Churchill and I hope I do not sound presumptuous if I add that he won mine also. Recently I borrowed one of the two copies of Blackadder's *Life and Diary*[9] from the Ministry of Defence library. It has given me profitable and interesting reading.

Blackadder would have regarded his diary as a spiritual register of his experience, not intended to see the light of day, and therefore it is a faithful transcription of his inner life. Providentially, some years after his death Blackadder's letters to his wife and the diary came into the hands of a tobacconist who had an eye for business and sold them to a Christian writer. In 1799 the hymn-writer, John Newton, then rector of St Mary's Lombard Street in London, agreed to write a recommendatory preface if they were printed, but it was not until 1824 that they were published under the masterly direction of a Mr Andrew Crichton. Thus a most valuable record of the experiences and the issues that faced a Christian officer in the early eighteenth century has been preserved for us today. The modern reader will soon observe, like the writer of Ecclesiastes, that 'there is nothing new under the sun.'[10]

Early Life

John Blackadder was born in Dumfriesshire in September 1664, the descendant of a Scottish baronetcy and the son of a Presbyterian minister who was also one of the first 'Field Preachers.' The father suffered sorely under the episcopal persecution,[11] was declared 'rebel and fugitive,' and was incarcerated in Bass Rock prison, where he died in 1655. However, he left behind him at least one son who inherited his father's simple trust in Christ. There is no record of any dramatic crisis conversion in John Blackadder's early life, but it is evident that by the age of twelve he had met God in Christ (to use Archbishop Temple's definition of a Christian), was trusting Him as Saviour, and was endeavouring to obey Him as Lord. Crichton comments: 'His piety, though early, proved uniform and abiding.'

In 1688, William III accepted the invitation to become King of England. This event changed young John Blackadder's temporal fortunes. By habit and education he was not suited to the military profession and, like many others since, his joining the Army may have been a matter of necessity rather than desire. We may note that he had no difficulty in reconciling his beliefs with his profession and in his preface Crichton provides an eloquent exposition of Biblical teaching on this issue. John Blackadder was accordingly commissioned into the Cameronians, 'a psalm-singing regiment,' which had guarded the Field Preachers' secret meetings in previous years.

Formative Years

The following year (1689) he had his first experience of action when his regiment faced the Highland Army at the Battle of Dunkeld. A letter to his brother written two hours after the battle reveals a humble dependence on God:

> *I must say the Lord's presence was most visible, strengthening us so that none of the glory belongs to us but to His own great name. It was not by might, or our power, nor conduct (our best officers were killed or disabled) so that we have many things to humble us, and to make us trust and eye Him above, and not instruments. I pray God help me not to forget such a mercy I have met with.*

The diary includes events that may appear humorous to the modern reader. One Sunday on board a troopship, Blackadder sought a place of solitude for his daily period of Bible reading and prayer. Seeing the ship was becalmed, he climbed the mast to the crow's nest. Alas, his devotions were disturbed when, without warning, a fierce storm blew up and he had to make a speedy descent as the ship's company hurriedly raised the sails and the ship sped forth for 140 miles at best speed! On another occasion he narrowly escaped being killed by one of his men who negligently discharged his musket while cleaning it!

His Character

Blackadder faced many issues which have a ring of familiarity to Christian officers of this generation. He was by nature introspective and quiet. He was aware of the dangers of worldly company with its tendency to cool a man's love for Christ. As he got older and more senior in rank he noticed that this danger did not diminish. Fortunately, in his early life he realised the importance of both private and public worship. Every day, even on extended marches, he found time for Bible reading and prayer. He memorised key verses, especially the promises of God to His believing children, and then would claim them in prayer, judging that he was approaching his Master on ground He had covenanted to bless. It grieved Blackadder when military duty prevented him from attending a service. He took communion regularly ('I took hold of Christ in my heart, and fed upon Him by faith'). He did not hesitate to lay professional matters before the Lord and saw his prayers abundantly answered in operations, training, and administration. At times it saddened him to see ungodly men prosper. 'I see the greatest rakes are the best recruiters,' he recorded sorrowfully during a tour as a recruiting officer.

Blackadder appears to have prayed regularly for his men. He never held a light view of sin, especially blasphemy and drunkenness, and he had the moral courage to issue appropriate rebukes.

'I fear sinning,' he wrote to a senior Christian officer, 'though you know I do not fear fighting.'

Marriage

In 1702 Blackadder married a Scottish Christian woman who shared his own simple faith. It is noteworthy that they had regular times of prayer together and when Blackadder was away during ten campaigning seasons they wrote to each other frequently. Unfortunately, they were not blessed with children but their affection for each other was in no way reduced and their marriage was abundantly happy. During the campaigning seasons of the War of the Spanish Succession, Mrs Blackadder took accommodation in Holland in order to be as close to her husband as acceptable. Their winters were always spent together.

Operational Experience

Perhaps the greatest value of Blackadder's diary for our own day is the artless testimony it provides to the power of Christ to keep a soldier efficient in his duty on operations when fighting in a just cause. This truth is one which our pacifist friends are reluctant to face.

Blackadder had no doubt at all that the British cause in the War of the Spanish Succession was just. The opulent, ambitious, and aggressive Louis XIV and his armies threatened both the balance of power in Europe and the freedom and livelihood of nations unable to protect themselves. When the war broke out, Blackadder records taking a solitary walk:

> I renewed my covenant with Christ and ratified whatever I had done before. I implored for such measures of grace as I should from time to time, stand in need of; and that He would supply sufficient strength and furniture, and order all my ways and actions aright.

The way the Lord honoured this simple act of faith is especially evident in the major battles of the war, each of which Blackadder describes as an *Ebenezer* ('Thus far the Lord has helped us').[12]

Blenheim

After the epic march down the Rhine with Marlborough in 1704 and the storming of Schellenberg, Captain Blackadder and the Cameronians took part in the victory at the Battle of Blenheim. In spite of a minor wound in the throat, he recorded in his diary that evening:

> ...*I was enabled to exercise a lively faith, relying and encouraging myself in God, whereupon I was easy, sedate and cheerful... During all the little intervals of action, I kept looking to God for strength and courage, and had [plenty], both to keep my own heart and help to discharge my duty well in station...*

Winston Churchill's account reveals his delight in Blackadder's inspiring leadership and the response of his men.

Ramillies

Two years later Blackadder, recently promoted to Major by Marlborough, for whom he had a great affection and respect, was involved in the Battle of Ramillies. He noted with perhaps a degree of Scottish partisanship that the English ('the boldest sinners in the Army') had only a small part in the victory and judged that God had used others as His instruments in order to humble the pride of the English. This sentiment would surely have brought a wry smile to the face of Winston Churchill, that most English of Englishmen, as he read this passage of Blackadder's diary! Nevertheless, he generously applauds 'the valiant major's piety.'[13] Of himself Blackadder recorded 'I was easy and helped to discharge my duty well.'

Oudenarde

The year 1707 was the one in which Blackadder was involved more in combat than in any other in his military career. And yet after the Battle of Oudenarde he wrote:

> *This is another Ebenezer of my life to be added to Blenheim, Ramillies etc. We fought the French and by the mercy of God*

beat them. I was liberally supplied with courage, resolution and a calm mind. All is the gift of God... My frame was more spiritual and serene than ordinary. My thoughts were much upon the 103rd Psalm ('Bless the Lord, O my soul, and all that is within me, bless His holy name'[14]) which I sang (in my heart) frequently upon the march.

Two months later, Major Blackadder was ordered to undertake a perilous operation involving an assault on a counterscarp[15] with 400 men at the Siege of Lisle. I could not help noting with interest that the promises from Scripture that Blackadder claimed for himself as he faced this challenge were almost identical to those I had committed to memory as a boy and as a young officer (Joshua 1:9, Isaiah 41:10, Isaiah 43:1–5, Psalm 91, and Hebrews 13:5). In spite of being wounded in both the head and an arm, his mission was accomplished and he was able to write a day or so later to his wife thanking the Lord for His sustenance and mercy.

Malplaquet

Perhaps Blackadder's finest hours were at the battle of Malplaquet in 1709, after which he wrote:

I never was more secure and easy... It was the most deliberate, solemn and well-ordered battle that I ever saw – a noble and fine disposition, and as nobly executed. Every man was at his post; and I never saw troops engage with more cheerfulness, boldness and resolution. In all the soldiers' faces appeared a brisk and lively gaiety that presaged victory. The Lord of Hosts went forth at our head as Captain of our host, and the Army followed with a daring, cheerful boldness, for we never doubted that we would beat them... For my own part I was nobly and richly supplied as I always had been on such occasions, with liberal supplies of grace and strength, as the exigencies of the day called for. I never had a more pleasant day in my life. I was kept in perfect peace; my mind stayed, trusting in God... I did not seek any assurance or protection for my life; I thought it enough to believe in general, to depend with resignation, and hang about His land... Not unto us, O Lord, be the glory but to Thyself. It was not our sword or our bow, but it was the Lord's doing.

In the course of the victory, Major Blackadder had the disappointment of seeing his Commanding Officer killed close to him. This led to a personal crisis with echoes in our own time. Sir Winston Churchill's sympathetic description of the events that followed can scarcely be surpassed:

> Colonel Cranston's death made a vacancy to which Major Blackadder had claims. The faithful officer waited upon the Duke, composing himself with pious dignity. He knew that promotion cometh neither from the east nor from the west, nevertheless his diary and letters to his wife show a natural anxiety. The claimants were busy and pressing, and he feared lest influence and favour should outstrip him. If so, he was resigned. 'Let others, whose talent it is, get places and posts by assurance and forwardness. I shall have mine by modesty or want them, for I cannot force nature... This winter probably will make you either a Lieutenant Colonel's lady or a farmer's wife... But valour was rewarded; all was well. Merit prevailed. Providence, acting through Marlborough's hands, guarded his interests. In October, he was promoted to command of the Cameronians in which famous regiment his name should live.

Influence in Retirement

The Treaty of Utrecht was signed in 1711 and, apart from commanding the Glasgow Regiment in the defeat of the Old Pretender in 1716, Blackadder's military service was over. He sold his commission. However, his years as a retired officer were well used and influential. His diary reveals many wise observations. For example, although he was a patriotic Scot himself, he was aware that passion and godly zeal are not synonymous, especially in religious debate. 'I wish men were more warm-hearted and cooler-headed in religion,' he recorded after a Kirk Session.

Blackadder figured prominently in public life and was well aware of its perils. He became Deputy Governor of Stirling Castle and was a member of the General Assembly. He had clear, balanced, and orthodox Biblical beliefs. Doctrinally, his convictions were probably identical to those of that great contemporary Scottish divine, Samuel Rutherford. Blackadder rightly abhorred teaching that took men into legalism and self-righteousness or antinomianism (which holds that the moral law of God is not binding on Christians).

More positively, he held a strong doctrine of the Christian's assurance of salvation through faith in the atoning work of Christ. As he wrote, 'A bold assurance is quite consistent with a humble and needy reliance upon Him.' He detested party politics and his advice to Synod when preparing to appoint a minister involved in a dispute is perceptive and spiritual:

> *...Let them join together and choose a faithful, pious, peaceable Gospel minister; a man far from party-spirit, for I will venture to say, the Gospel never did, and never will, thrive in the hands of a party man. Advise them to choose a man who has no other end in view, but to lead them to Christ; in a word a man that can say on his admission 'For I determined to know nothing among you except Jesus Christ, and Him crucified,'[16] and at the close of his*

The Battle of Malplaquet, 11th September 1709. Oil on canvas by Louis Laguerre (1663-1721), 1713 (c). To the right, Marlborough gives orders to his troops whilst fighting continues in the background.

ministry can say with the Apostle 'For our proud confidence is this: the testimony of our conscience, that in holiness and godly sincerity, not in fleshly wisdom but in the grace of God, we have conducted ourselves in the world, and especially toward you.'[17]

Closing Comments

This biographical note must not be open to the charge of 'saint worship.' Were there no points at which this gallant Christian officer was weak? His critics no doubt would have accused him of being unsociable and distant, but this is an easy charge to make at the expense of those who take seriously 'holiness without which no man shall see the Lord.'[18] The balance of being, 'in the world but not of it,' is an elusive one.

If there is a defect in his witness to Christ which emerges from his diary it is a surprising one and I only venture to mention it so that we can learn from it. He records singularly few attempts to commend by word of mouth the Master he loved to his fellow men, especially to his soldiers. It seems that he found it easier to condemn his unregenerate contemporaries for their profligacy and unbelief than to encourage them to repent and trust in Christ. However, like us, he lived in an age of open sin and our criticism of him must not be overstated.

Lieutenant Colonel John Blackadder was an officer who fought the good fight of faith. He endeavoured to live 'sensibly, righteously and godly in the present age.'[19] May the Lord raise up others like him in our own day and generation, for his life is a testimony to the faithfulness of God.

6

CH Malan, Officer and Evangelist

A Soldier's Experience of God's Love and Faithfulness

Edited by Philip Bray

In July 1857 Captain Charles Hamilton Malan boarded a Royal Navy ship bound for India, where the Indian Mutiny had begun two months previously.[20] Such journeys could last well over a year and were often full of adventure. However, this journey started so smoothly that some of the officers began to complain; it was more like a coastal cruise than the adventure they had all anticipated. This quickly changed when the ship was suddenly hit by gale-force winds that shredded the topsails before the crew could lower them. The masts were snapped off 'as twigs' and the ship listed hard. For a moment, it seemed that she would not recover and that they would be lost. Malan was responsible for the prisoners and their guard and, having seen to his duties, stood on deck next to the Captain. It took all of his strength just to hold on.

The Captain leaned over and with cupped hands shouted into his ear, 'You are in greater danger now than ever you were at Sebastopol. If the foresail goes, we shall all go to the bottom.'[21]

Malan was commissioned into the 7th Fusiliers, City of London Regiment and later the 75th Stirlingshire Gordon Highlanders. His early years of service in the Army had been eventful. In his first appointment, in command of a platoon of 30 men, he had fought in and narrowly escaped death at the Battle of Sebastopol in the Crimean War. Many of his unit were killed, including his Commanding Officer.

He was a religious man who read the Bible every day and tried to obey it. He thought he could be accepted by God on the basis of his obedience. Now, in the midst of the storm, when the ship's survival hung in the balance, Malan's eyes were suddenly opened. Surveying a scene of devastation, he realised that he was not only in *temporal* danger but also, and far more seriously, he was in *eternal* danger. 'I saw death, judgment, and eternity before me as I never before had seen them. I also saw in the raging of the wind and sea... His power against Him to whom I knew myself to be a sinner.'

Finally, the storm passed and the ship and her crew escaped. However, Malan's sense of his eternal danger would not pass. When a brother officer invited Malan to pray with him in his cabin and to thank God for their deliverance, Malan eagerly accepted. Kneeling down, Malan fervently confessed his sin and asked the Lord for mercy 'and in due time I received pardon and peace… ignorant as I was, I asked and sought, and I did not do so in vain.' He left the cabin a new man. Like the calm that had followed the passing of the storm, an inner peace and conviction that God's anger had also passed from him came to Malan. He described it as 'the peace of free, full, and eternal forgiveness of sins through the blood of Christ.' This peace never left him and the experience was so real to him that, from that moment, he tirelessly sought to bring others to the same free forgiveness through the blood of Christ. He had the great privilege of seeing many other soldiers and sailors turning to Christ.

Joy Throughout Heaven

After a few years in India Malan fell ill and was sent back to England on board a troop ship to recover. Soon after his conversion, he was advised never to delay in speaking to others about Christ. Therefore, Malan ventured below deck to speak to the sailors and passengers. 'What encouragement the Lord gave me the very first day!'

The sides of the hull were lined with sick and dying men. He walked amongst them speaking a warm word to each of them about the man's regiment and then, standing in the centre of the cabin, addressed them: 'Comrades, let me read to you the Word of God. Whether in sickness or health, joy or sorrow, this blessed book is our best friend.' He then explained how he had come to Christ in the storm and offered to read to them from the Bible. Some propped themselves up in their beds so that they could hear. He took for his text the story of the Prodigal Son:

> *Here we learn that the love of God gives free and full forgiveness of sins to the sinner who turns to Him. The father kissed his son, in token of his acceptance before the son could say, 'Father, I have sinned.' Because sin had been atoned for, put away by the blood and sacrifice of Christ, God forgives the guiltiest sinner who turns*

to Him before he can get on his knees and confess his sins! His forgiveness was purchased when his great Substitute died for him. He can rejoice in his forgiveness when he believes that the Substitute was the Son of God, who lives in glory to bring him there. Then, while he rejoices, he will mourn that he should have so long rejected one who so loved him. This is repentance, because he will then forsake sin and turn to God.

He had just returned to the deck, exhausted by his long day's work and first venture for the Gospel, when a Corporal called to him and said that one of the prisoners, a deserter called McNiff, wanted to speak to him privately.

'Sir,' McNiff said, 'I'm a great sinner. I've done very wrong, and I'm very, very sorry for it. I heard what you read this afternoon, and I am like that poor man. You said there was mercy for all who repent. I do most truly; will God forgive me?' I took his hand. It was pitch dark, but I felt God was present. 'My poor friend, you are causing joy through all heaven.'

The prisoner, still lying in his bed, called to God for forgiveness and soon received the same perfect peace of conscience that Malan had received. Although, naturally, he was in a desperate state, facing death by consumption or, if he lived, severe punishment in Britain as a deserter, his final days were full of joy and peace. Malan visited him daily and, when the man did eventually succumb to disease, conducted his sea burial. At the very moment when he committed the body to the deep, a wave came right up to the very edge of the gangway and the body just slipped quietly into the water without even a splash. Malan took this as a sign that this former sinner had been absolutely forgiven through Christ and was received by Him, 'with the tenderness of a mother to her child.'

This first experience of witnessing the grace of God to forgive and change great sinners left an indelible impression on Malan. From that moment he always prayed that God would give him further opportunities to speak of Christ and he was tireless in their pursuit, as one further incident illustrates.

* * *

A typical scene of wounded men lying on the floor of a British field dressing station probably immediately after the Battle of Modder River in 1899.

In 1868 Malan was promoted to the rank of Major and was placed in command of a company of around 100 men in Hong Kong. Possibly because he had already been invalided from India and because Chinese summers had a fearful reputation for disease, he dreaded the assignment. However, having publicly declared his absolute trust in Christ, he dared not turn down the posting in case Christ should also be dishonoured.

Therefore, as they set sail from England to Hong Kong, Malan prayed earnestly. After a short while his prayer seemed to have been answered when a Bible text came with assurance to his heart, '"take courage," declares the Lord, "and work; for I am with you," declares the Lord of hosts.'[22]

The ship's Captain was a personal friend and gave him permission to visit the sailors and to speak to them about Christ. Malan visited the various dining rooms and offered to read the Bible to them every evening. His offer was received warmly and every day for the next sixteen months Malan read and explained the Scriptures to the ship's crew from half-past six until eight o'clock and in the afternoons he read the Bible to the sick in the hospital.

A year or more after the voyage, he met one of the sailors who had been on the same ship and the sailor told him how he too had come to believe in Jesus Christ and had received the forgiveness of sins. He recounted:

> *I was lying in my hammock in fear and trembling when I saw you come down to read the Gospel to the men. I could not hear a word you said, but I could see your face and I watched you the whole time. I saw your bright, happy smile just the same as ever. I said to myself, 'Here am I, an old sailor, many years at sea, and I am afraid now in this gale; and here's a landsman as happy as if he were ashore.' I felt that you had what I had not; I felt that you had, what I had heard you say you had, forgiveness of sins and eternal life. I prayed that night. Ever afterwards I came near you when you were reading, and when I left the ship I was a believer in the Lord Jesus Christ.*

Malan did indeed remember the gale! The last thing he had wanted to do was to go below deck, but he decided that if he did not, the men would think that he was afraid and that the God whom he was proclaiming was actually no help in a crisis. It would have been

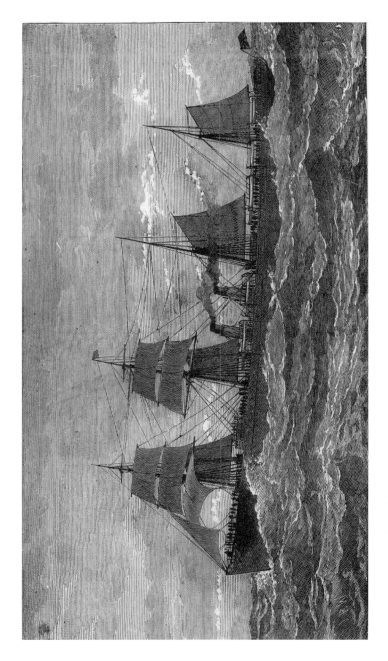

Etching of a troopship, the *Spain*, carrying reinforcements to the Zulu War in 1879

tantamount to saying that there was no God. Therefore, clinging to the mess table while the ship was tossed from side to side, he addressed them, saying, 'The Word of God is the same in a storm as in a calm, men; it always does us good' and set about explaining a passage from the Bible. He had not realised that as he spoke his face was radiant and this had made such an impression on some of his hearers, including this sailor, that it had been the first step in their conversion. A little step of faith had been used by God to eternal good.

After these sixteen months of work for Christ, he arrived in India, no longer full of anxiety at the dangers that lay ahead, but with a heart that was 'rejoicing in God more than it had ever done before.' Malan had learned that men's souls are of such incomparable value that there is no greater duty or anything more fulfilling than telling others about Christ.

I Know Whom I Have Believed

Over the years a second desire began to develop in his heart, perhaps shaped by seeing the effect of his conduct on the sailors during the storm. He started to pray that God would place him in command of a body of men in a position of great danger and then deliver them. Whereas before and immediately after his conversion he was afraid when trouble came, he had learned that he could trust God absolutely. He now actively sought danger.

He expected that his prayer would be answered by God's saving him in the heat of a great battle. However, in the Lord's great wisdom He chose to answer Malan's prayer in a more unexpected but no less miraculous manner, in October 1871 in South Africa.

From the moment that Malan and his men landed in South Africa it rained. They arrived on a Wednesday in the rain; it then rained on the Thursday and even harder on the Friday. Having travelled from China and its harsh climate, his men were weak and highly vulnerable to disease.

By the Saturday morning their camp was awash and something had to be done urgently. However, the more it rained, the more Malan prayed, until he received a calm assurance that God would answer. Then, quite suddenly, after breakfast on Saturday he felt impelled to go into the nearby town with a few others to find better shelter. Before setting out, he prayed that God would open the heart of anyone who might have a suitable building. The very first person they met had a suitable property and offered it to them, remarking that he had been thinking how the soldiers must have been suffering in the weather after China. This was exactly the right solution to his problem; the man's heart had been opened and the building was large enough to house 300 soldiers. Malan returned to camp with a light heart, rejoicing that his prayer had been answered.

Barely had the soldiers settled into the building before an even more intense storm broke and continued all night. The soldier whom they had left to guard the camp reported that the whole of it was now ankle-deep in water. A ship had been wrecked just off the coast and even the harbour-master remarked that it was the worst weather he had seen in 28 years. Malan recognised that they had indeed been in great danger but God had answered his prayer and delivered them.

However, having returned to camp on the Sunday, when they awoke on the Monday, ready for a twenty-mile march to King William's Town, they were greeted by the sound of rain. The danger had not completely passed! Malan realised that if they now spent all day soaked to the skin they would lose all of the benefit of sheltering in the village. Once again Malan prayed and, as he did so, a Bible verse came into his heart: 'Elijah was a man with a nature like ours, and he prayed earnestly that it would not rain, and it did not rain on the earth for three years and six months.'[23]

He took this as his answer, rose, threw his cloak over his shoulder, and prayed: '"Where is the Lord, the God of Elijah."[24] O Lord, hear!' At that moment he heard an officer in a nearby tent ask his assistant if there were any changes to the orders in light of the worsening weather. Malan answered the officer himself with a firm 'no,' stepped out of his tent, walked over to the Sergeant-Major's tent, and told him to have the company fall in to begin the march. Before Malan returned to his own tent, the rain had stopped. Though heavy thunder-clouds hung ominously above them and at times seemed to be just metres above their heads, not one drop of rain fell on them throughout the day's march. He continued to pray for his men throughout the march, asking God for strength and, although it was a tough journey, not even the oldest soldier collapsed. Two weeks later one of his officers commented, 'Well, Major, that was a very wonderful thing; we have just talked about it. All that rain at East London, and not a man caught a cold!' Malan knew just how wonderful it was; God had given him his desire and delivered his men out of great danger.

A typical British Army tented camp in Africa in 1868.

CH Malan's sword inscribed with his name.

The Final Act of Love to a Soldier

While the Regiment was in Hong Kong a complaint had been made against Malan. It was alleged that Malan had treated two soldiers unfairly. Although it seems that the two soldiers bore a grudge against Malan, having been disciplined by him, Malan's Commanding Officer was required by military law to refer the matter back to Army Headquarters. The investigation broadened in its scope and finally, after some months of investigation, a decision was dispatched to the Regiment while it was still in South Africa. It contained a hammer blow; Malan was ordered to stop speaking to his soldiers about Christ:

> *I have to request that Major Malan may be informed that it is not within his province to impart religious instruction to the soldiers under his command, and that he must discontinue the distribution of tracts of any religious tendency among them.*

Of all the storms which Malan faced, this must have seemed the hardest and was possibly the most unexpected. He could continue to serve but must cease all work for Christ unless he was to disobey a direct order, which Malan would not consider. Rather than being discouraged or bitter, in his journal he describes the decision as God's, 'final act of love to a soldier.' Four incidents confirmed to him that God was in fact in full control and was using this hard trial for Malan's good.

First, Malan had a final opportunity to speak to his soldiers about Christ just before he received the decision and it was a most wonderful occasion. As was his pattern on Sundays, he went to the hospital to visit the sick soldiers and to speak to them about Christ:

> *Yes, my dear comrades, if we do what Mary did – if we believe in the Lord Jesus as Saviour and Lord – if we sit at His feet and hear His words, the world may do what it likes. We may lose health, wealth, or position; we may lose friends, or whatever we hold most dear on earth – we have chosen, by God's grace, that good part, which shall not be taken from us.*

Little did he think that in just a few hours his dearest treasure on earth was to be taken from him; the privilege of telling his soldiers about the free forgiveness available in Christ through the love of God.

Secondly, later the same day Malan attended a church meeting and was unusually comforted by the text that the visiting speaker chose. He immediately remembered the verse when he received the decision and he made it his own prayer: 'It is the Lord; let Him do what seems good to Him.' [25]

Thirdly, it was the responsibility of the Garrison Commander, who was a Christian and dear friend, to notify Malan of the decision. Therefore, a most crushing blow was somewhat softened by being delivered by a close friend and believer. Malan wrote, 'a friend told me that a letter had come... a friend's voice prepared me for its contents, and a friend's hand gave it to me to read.'

Finally, as one door of ministry seemed to be irrevocably shutting, another door was opening. Just before he received the decision, Malan had been invited to visit a mission station and while there the missionary was called back to Scotland to see his dying father. He asked Malan to cover for him. Malan was struck by the remarkable response that the Gospel was having and by the urgent need for labourers. Just as his ability to serve Christ in the military seemed to be ending, another door opened.

These four events led Malan to conclude that God was indeed working out the consequences for good of even this seemingly tragic storm and that He was calling Malan out of the Army to a new work. But his army work was not quite finished.

The Tenderness of God

A few weeks after the decision had been given to Malan, the General in command of all British Forces on the Cape of Good Hope came to inspect Malan's unit. The General had a formidable reputation for his battlefield experience and 'indefatigable exertions in rifle instruction.' He had commanded a Regiment for an astonishing nineteen years. Malan's men were to conduct a manoeuvre on the square and then the General would inspect their administrative processes and records. Malan met for special prayer with the Commandant and they asked that God would greatly help.

On the morning of the inspection, Malan sat in his garden reading the Bible. He turned to the Psalms and read, 'I cling to Your testimonies; O Lord, do not put me to shame!'[26] The words seemed to sum up his whole situation and prayer. He closed the book with a shout of joy, assured that God had answered their prayers.

When the General came to inspect the unit's bank accounts, he was astonished. Normally soldiers wasted their money on drink and, rather than depositing money *in* the bank, were debtors *to* the bank. However, when he inspected the first company he found that they had very few debtors and a lot of depositors. He could scarcely believe his eyes and went to the next company, where he found the same situation. 'Well,' said the General, 'I never saw anything like this before in my life.'

When Malan first arrived in South Africa, although exhausted from his time in the Far East, he had been deeply troubled by the prevalence of drunkenness. Brandy was cheaper in South Africa than beer in England. Accordingly, many soldiers were drunkards. At first, Malan did not have the strength to address the problem, but for three days he made it a matter of prayer and then went around the camp, speaking to the Regiment and begging them not to waste their lives on alcohol.

The bank balances were proof that a miraculous change had taken place. The General was so surprised by what he found that he turned to his assistant and asked 'did you ever see anything like this?' The General concluded his inspection by addressing the Regiment:

> *I have never been more surprised in all my life than by what I have seen today… I expected to find a lot of sickly, rheumatic old men, instead of which I find a body of young and healthy soldiers.*

As Malan accompanied the General back across the parade square, his eyes filled with tears as he realised that God had seen his suffering and heard his prayers. After a while the General turned to him and said:

> *Well, Major, I must honestly tell you that I have never been so mistaken in any man as I have been in you… I came up here thoroughly prejudiced against you. The Horse Guards' correspondence, reports I had heard about you, etc., made me expect to find another state of things. I assure you I think very differently now… I had expected to find everything in confusion, your officers discontented, and your men – why, I find everything*

*in perfect order; everybody happy. I never saw such a happy body
of men before in my life.*

Then, as though this were not enough, he pleaded with Malan
to stay in the Army and offered to write to the Army Headquarters
on his behalf.

A Better Work

An elderly Christian once said that 'there is no greater honour than
to be a servant of Christ. It is a greater honour than even to be a
Field Marshal in Her Majesty's Army.' Malan chose this honour.
Despite the General's kind words, the *London Gazette* records that
on 17th July 1872 Major CH Malan retired from military service.
Little else is recorded of the work he undertook at the South African
mission station.

Malan is a great example of single-mindedness, prayerfulness,
and humble faith in God but above all his story shows the wonderful
goodness of God; He is a God who freely forgives all who come to
Him through the blood of His Son and then equips them for a life
of joyful service.

While Malan of course had faults, as we all do, it was a mark
of his godliness that, rather than cease to proclaim the Gospel, he
chose to resign his commission.

Malan had one final desire. He wrote, 'It is my special desire that
these notes of God's dealings with me as a soldier may be useful to old
soldiers, whether they served as officers or in the ranks.' Doubtless
he would give his full approval for his account to be published anew
for our generation.

7

DL Moody: a Willing Offering

From the Official Biography by WR Moody

Edited by Michael Claydon

And the people blessed all the men who volunteered...
Nehemiah 11:2

Dwight Lyman Moody was an American evangelist based in Chicago who lived from 1837 until 1899. Despite never having enlisted in the army, he willingly gave himself to the service of soldiers by bringing them the good news of the Gospel. Whether personally witnessing to an individual soldier or organising and encouraging others, Moody used every means possible to tell men facing battle of the one true answer to every man's greatest need. His influence on the American and British military was profound. The Soldiers' Christian Association resulted from a series of Gospel meetings held by Moody in London in 1887 at which a number of soldiers were converted.

Born on 5th February 1837 in Northfield, Massachusetts into a farming family, Moody had to work from an early age because his father died young. As Moody grew up, he became restless at the rural life and moved to Boston, where he eventually found a job in his uncle's shoe shop with his terms of service requiring attendance at a Sunday school Bible class.

Through the teaching and witnessing of the class teacher, Moody accepted Christ and experienced a complete transformation. Whereas previously he had been living a passive religious life restricted by moral law where church attendance was a duty, Moody now found his greatest joy to be the service of his God. As he expressed it, 'Before my conversion, I worked towards the Cross, but since then I have worked from the Cross; then I worked to be saved, now I work because I am saved.' This was the beginning of a remarkable ministry that spanned the globe, with some estimating that Moody preached to as many as 100 million people.

Moody gave up his life as a successful businessman in order to devote himself to the preaching of the Gospel in 1860, just one year before the American Civil War began. Therefore, much of his early ministry was amongst soldiers and lessons learnt on this particular 'battlefield' were applied throughout the rest of his ministry.

He and many other Christians in Chicago were moved by the urgent need of the soldiers to hear the Gospel. At times, up to 12,000 soldiers were garrisoned on the outskirts of the city, many of whom were already fatally injured and others would be killed on the battlefields soon afterwards. A group of Christians under the leadership of Moody, did everything in their power to ensure that not one soldier died without hearing of Christ.

This chapter is based on an extract from Moody's official biography, which he commissioned his son to write. Moody 'willingly offered himself' to serve his Lord and Saviour. It is exciting to hear how the Lord used such obedience and how mightily He moved amongst members of the Army. It stands as an encouragement to us that, even today, the same Lord can do the same in the Armed Forces.

* * *

Civil War and the Beginning of a Military Ministry

The American Civil war started in 1861 with the Confederate forces firing on Fort Sumter. Camp Douglas was formed near the southern limits of Chicago and there recruits underwent military training. Among these new soldiers were a large number of 'Moody's boys' from the North Market Hall, the Sunday school that Moody had pioneered. A company was also raised among his friends and former business associates; on all sides he was urged to enter the service of his country.

Moody was strongly for the cause of the Union, with both his upbringing and training strongly supporting the abolition of slavery. In spite of all this, he could not in good conscience enlist. 'There has never been a time in my life when I felt that I could take a gun and shoot down a fellow-being. In this respect I am a Quaker.' At the same time, he was alive to the opportunity for doing good that the military camps offered and at once assisted in forming an Army and Navy Committee of the Young Men's Christian Association.

The first Christian work undertaken by the commission consisted of services held among the soldiers that passed through Chicago. On the forming of Camp Douglas, a work party was organised which resulted in the building of a small, temporary chapel in which over 1,500 meetings were held.

Moody's approach was inventive and sought to make the most of every opportunity for getting the good news of the Gospel to the soldiers. One of his fellow workers, Edgar W Hawley, describes the beginning of this work:

> At one time there were about 12,000 men there. Regiments were coming in and others going to the front all the time. The Young Men's Christian Association had a chapel for the use of the men, where frequent meetings were held. We issued an 'Army Hymn Book' with an American flag on the front page, and it was distributed freely among the soldiers. We visited the tents and barracks and found the men playing cards and proposed to exchange our hymn-books for the cards. The soldiers agreed quickly enough; indeed, so numerous were these exchanges that several of the Young Men's Christian Association rooms were full of playing-cards which the men had surrendered.

Ministry Amongst Prisoners of War

With all the newly trained soldiers deployed, Camp Douglas had completed its role as a training base. Following the capture of around 9,000 Confederate soldiers at Fort Donelson, the base was used as a prisoner-of-war camp with a Union regiment as guards. Moody was not slow to make the most of this opportunity. Hawley describes one particular event following the close of a prayer meeting:

> 'Hawley, let us go down and hold a meeting there in the chapel with the prisoners.' As we neared the entrance to the camp Moody said, 'Here is a ministerial pass; take it.' 'But how will you get in past the guard?' I asked. 'In some way,' was the confident reply!
> The guard passed me right in, but Moody was halted by fixed bayonets. 'Stand back,' came the stern order. 'I am Moody, the president of the Young Men's Christian Association,' he explained to the soldier. 'I don't care who you are; you can't get in here!' At that moment a Captain who was passing stepped up and recognised the evangelist. To him Moody appealed. 'Let me in,' he urged, 'for the work's sake.' The officer turned to the guard. 'Let one of your men take Moody to headquarters; I will be responsible.' We marched to the headquarters, Moody under military guard. On hearing the explanation, the officer in charge said, 'Well, seeing

DL Moody portrait in 1862.

you are here, and considering your object, you may stay, but don't repeat it. If you are not out of here by eight p.m. you go into the guard-house for the night.'

We went to the chapel, arranged things, and invited the men. It was soon packed full. Turning to me with a twinkle in his eye, Moody said 'Now, Hawley, you preach.' I remonstrated and said I wasn't a minister. 'But you came in on a ministerial pass and I didn't.' He persisted and so I quietly acquiesced and we had an interesting service. Moody took charge and it seemed as though the Spirit of the Lord came down upon these men with great power. They came forward to the altar – 20, 30, and 40 at a time.

We closed the meeting and began answering individuals' questions. Moody had the platform and God used him wonderfully. The whole audience melted and we saw strong men in tears. 'God is here!' Moody whispered to me. When we finally looked at our watches it was a few seconds before eight and we had to run to get out of camp, having no desire to pass the night in the guard-house.

These meetings we kept up two or three weeks and many were converted. We formed a Young Men's Christian Association branch at the camp and there were many kind expressions of gratitude even from the higher officers, who were greatly pleased with the work.

Moody's Tactics

By means of Gospel services, prayer meetings, song services, distribution of Bibles, books, and tracts, and by individual conversations, Moody tried to win the soldiers to Christ. His aim was not merely to make converts: instead, he was obedient to the great commission to 'make disciples.' He sought to build up and encourage the Christians by organising them into 'Bands of Brothers,' who were to carry 'the Banner of Christ' with them and be loyal to one another and to their Divine Captain. In a letter to his mother early in the war, Moody's bond with the soldiers and his love for his Saviour is shown:

I am now at work among the soldiers a good deal. The boys wanted to have me become their chaplain, but my friends would not let me go, so I shall remain in the city. I would like to see you all and talk with you about my Saviour, who seems so near to me. Oh, what would life be without Christ! I sometimes get to looking down on this world of sin, but when I look to Jesus it makes me look up.

Nor was Moody's ministry limited to the training camps. While Moody was serving under the command of General OO Howard, who was in thorough sympathy with his efforts, Moody's ministry was especially fruitful. Here General Howard describes Moody's work in the army:

Moody and I met for the first time in Cleveland, East Tennessee. It was about the middle of April, 1864. I was bringing together my Fourth Army Corps. Two divisions had already arrived and were encamped in and near the village. Moody was then fresh and hearty, full of enthusiasm for the Master's work. Our soldiers were just about to set out on what we all felt promised to be a hard and bloody campaign and I think we were especially desirous of strong preaching. Crowds and crowds turned out to hear him. He showed them how a soldier could give his heart to God. His preaching was direct and effective and multitudes responded with a promise to follow Christ.

An Urgent Appeal

The immediate threat to life made it necessary to urge his hearers to accept immediate salvation. Whether with severely injured men 'hovering between life and death' or men briefly resting on a long march, it was a choice of 'now or never.' As Moody would not allow himself to be satisfied with 'never,' he put all his effort into 'now.'

Although Moody would not bear arms, he went wherever the Gospel was needed and was on the ground ministering to the wounded after the battles of Pittsburg Landing, Shiloh, and Murfreesboro. It was after one of these battles that the following incident occurred, as Moody here describes:

We were taking a large number of wounded men down the Tennessee River after the battle of Pittsburg Landing. A number of

*young men of the Christian Commission were with me, and I told
them that we must not let a man die on the boat that night without
telling him of Christ and Heaven.*

*You know the cry of a wounded man is 'Water! Water!' As we
passed along from one to another giving them water, we tried to
tell them of the Water of Life, of which if they would drink they
would never die. I came to one man who had about as fine a face
as I ever saw. I spoke to him, but he did not answer. I went to the
doctor and said,*

*'Doctor, do you think that man will recover?' 'No, he lost so
much blood before we got to him on the field that he fainted while
we were amputating his leg. He will never recover,' was the reply.
I said, 'I can't find out his name and it seems a pity to let him die
without knowing who he is. Don't you think we can bring him
to?' 'You may give him a little brandy and water,' said the doctor,
'that will revive him if anything will.'*

*I sat down beside him and gave him brandy and water every
now and then. While I was waiting I said to a man nearby, 'Do you
know this man?' 'Oh, yes, that is my chum.' 'Has he a father and
mother living?' 'He has a widowed mother.' 'Has he any brothers
or sisters?' 'Two sisters; but he is the only son.' 'What is his name?'
'William Clark.'*

*I said to myself that I could not let him die without getting a
message for that mother. Presently he opened his eyes and I said
'William, do you know where you are?' He looked around a little
dazed and then said 'Oh, yes! I am on my way home to mother.'
'Yes, you are on your way home,' I said, 'but the doctor says you
won't reach your earthly home. I thought I'd like to ask you if
you had any message for your mother.' His face lighted up with
an unearthly glow as he said 'Oh, yes, tell my mother that I died
trusting in Jesus!' It was one of the sweetest messages I ever heard
in my life!*

On returning to Chicago, Moody at once looked up the widowed
mother and two sisters and delivered the message from the dying
soldier. As he was leaving the house, one of the sisters, only a child
at the time, came to him and gave him the small savings of her sister
and herself with the request that he purchase a Bible to give to some
soldier. When he went back to the front Moody related this incident,
asking who wanted that Bible, and there were many requests for it.

Another incident that Moody frequently repeated occurred after the battle of Murfreesboro.

I was stationed in the hospital. For two nights I had been unable to get rest, and being really worn out, on the third night I had lain down to sleep. About midnight I was called to see a wounded soldier who was very low. At first I tried to put the messenger off, but he told me that if I waited till morning it might be too late. So I went to the ward where I had been directed and found the man who had sent for me. I shall never forget his face as I saw it that night in the dim, uncertain candle-light. I asked what I could do for him and he said that he wanted me to 'help him to die.' I told him I would bear him in my arms into the Kingdom of God if I could, but I couldn't. Then I tried to preach the Gospel. He only shook his head and said 'He can't save me; I have sinned all my life.'

My thoughts went back to his loved ones in the North and I thought that even then his mother might be praying for her boy. I repeated promise after promise and prayed with the dying man, but nothing I said seemed to help him. Then I said that I wanted to read to him an account of an interview that Christ had one night while here on earth: an interview with a man who was anxious about his eternal welfare. I read from the third chapter of John, how Nicodemus came to the Master. As I read on, his eyes became riveted upon me and he seemed to drink in every syllable. When I came to the words 'As Moses lifted up the serpent in the wilderness, even so must the Son of Man be lifted up: that whosoever believeth in Him should not perish, but have eternal life,' he stopped me and asked 'Is that there?' 'Yes,' I said. 'Well,' he said, 'I never knew that was in the Bible. Read it again.' Leaning on his elbow on the side of the cot, he brought his hands together tightly and when I finished he exclaimed 'That's good! Won't you read it again?' Slowly I repeated the passage the third time. When I finished I saw that his eyes were closed and the troubled expression on his face had given way to a peaceful smile. His lips moved and I bent over him to catch what he was saying, and heard in a faint whisper 'As Moses lifted up – the serpent – in the wilderness, – even so – must the Son of Man be lifted up: – that whosoever – believeth in Him – should not perish, – but have eternal life.'

He opened his eyes and said 'That's enough; don't read any more.' Early next morning I again came to his cot, but it was empty. The attendant in charge told me that the young man had died peacefully and said that after my visit he had rested quietly, repeating to himself, now and then, that glorious proclamation: 'whoever believes in Him shall not perish, but have eternal life.'

By the time the Civil War ended in 1865, these wartime experiences had introduced Moody to a larger field by bringing him prominently before the whole country. The Young Men's Christian Association's noon prayer-meetings in Chicago had become a centre where he and his fellow-workers met and reported on their frequent excursions to the front. People from all over the north-west sent in requests for prayer at these meetings, on behalf of husbands, brothers, and sons. Moody went on to travel the world preaching the Gospel; however, his ministry in the military was not yet over.

The Spanish War

When the Spanish-American War broke out in 1898 and thousands of young men were again gathered into army camps, Moody's heart went out towards them with the same longing that had urged him on during the Civil War. He became chairman of the Evangelistic Department of the Army and Navy Christian Commission, whose method of work was fourfold:

1. The preaching of the Gospel by well-known ministers and evangelists, to whom the men would listen.

2. The placing of Young Men's Christian Association tents within reach of every regiment, where the men might go as a place of resort and where they would find good reading and writing materials.

3. The free distribution of Bibles, Testaments, hymn books, and other religious books.

4. The visiting of the sick and wounded in hospitals.

His experiences in the American Civil War helped him to recruit the churches in this new emergency. The following letter, which he wrote at this time, resulted in great blessing to thousands of soldiers in the great military camps during the summer of 1898:

> *30 years ago war clouds gathered over our land and the church of God was aroused as I have never seen it since in behalf of the young men of America. This interest expressed itself in the formation of the Christian Commission and everywhere efforts were made for the religious interests of the soldiers. Meetings were held everywhere and many a camp became the scene of a deep and effective revival, and for more than 30 years I have been continually meeting men who were converted in those army meetings.*
>
> *Now the dark shadow of war again rests upon our land. Is it not possible that God intends to use even the darkness of this evil for the blessing of the youth of this land; and while He has called us to become the instrument of His justice may He not have in store a season of revival for those who, brought face to face with danger and in realisation of the seriousness of life, may be reached, when at other times careless and indifferent? It seems to me that it is just the nick of time in which to reach thousands of young men with the Gospel, either through a Testament, a good book, or the spoken message. A minister in Philadelphia writes me that there is an excellent opportunity of doing good at Tampa and I have no doubt that other camps offer equally favourable conditions.*

Ministers such as R. A. Torrey were sent and an appeal was made for money to send books as well as men. Bibles, religious books, library books and a large number of the new *Army Hymn Book*, compiled by Ira D. Sankey, were sent.

The fruit of this work is illustrated in an account by Major Whittle of one of many incidents:

> *I called on a dying Lieutenant this morning, who said that he was turned to God at the first meeting held in the camp. I did not know about it at the time, but my heart was full of gratitude to God as the dying man's face lit up in recognition of me! His hot hand pressed mine as he drank in 'the one who comes to Me I will certainly not cast out,' and other Scripture passages. He told me that he did in his heart trust Christ. We sang to him 'My faith looks up to Thee,' and commended him to God in prayer. He has a wife and five children. He was a travelling man and unsaved up*

to the night of May 27ᵗʰ. The doctor said there was no help and that he would die today. If God has been pleased to use my coming here to save that one soul, I will praise Him through eternity.

* * *

Born of the Spirit

It is fitting to conclude with a quote from Moody. It reveals the certainty of his hope in his Lord and Saviour, the same certainty that led him to offer himself willingly as an evangelist to soldiers.

Some day you will read in the papers that DL Moody, of East Northfield, is dead. Don't you believe a word of it! At that moment I shall be more alive than I am now, I shall have gone up higher, that is all; out of this old clay tenement into a house that is immortal – a body that death cannot touch; that sin cannot taint; a body fashioned like His glorious body.

I was born of the flesh in 1837. I was born of the Spirit in 1856. That which is born of the flesh may die, that which is born of the Spirit will live forever.

DL Moody preaching to a large crowd.

8

Sir Henry Havelock, 1795–1857

The Soldiers' General

By John Pollock

In the early months of 1823 the East Indiaman *General Kyd* was sailing southwards off the west coast of Africa, on its three-month voyage from England round the Cape to Bengal. Among the junior officers on board was an obscure Subaltern, Henry Havelock. He was aged twenty-seven and, after nearly eight years on home duties, having missed the Battle of Waterloo by a month, he had exchanged from the Rifle Brigade into the 13th Light Infantry, being anxious to see some active service in India.

He was small, thin and wiry, but remarkably good-looking. Having, however, neither family influence nor a long purse, he was determined to rise by sheer professional efficiency, a somewhat thin hope in the early nineteenth century except for time of war. Encouraged by his company commander, the redoubtable and famed Harry Smith, he had burrowed deep into textbooks and drilled and disciplined his men with enthusiasm.

At the same time he had tasted the pleasures of his garrison towns, where good-looking young officers were much in demand at balls, routs and romps, and pretty girls loved bright uniforms. He also read widely, and having been educated at Charterhouse and then having tried his hand at the law, until a family quarrel through him on his own resources, his mind was supple and active.

Henry Havelock found himself welcomed on the *General Kyd* as one of the few officers who had troubled to learn both Hindustani and Persian. With India not far away others welcomed his tuition. Among them was another Subaltern of his own Regiment, James Gardner,[27] with whom he struck up a warm friendship. Gardner was a Christian, with the courage of his convictions. Havelock, though occasionally stirred by memories of a Bible-reading mother, long dead, and of precocious sermon making with future bishops and archdeacons in the dormitory at Charterhouse, possessed nothing but the lip-service religion typical of his contemporaries in the service.

As the friendship developed Gardner sought to bring Havelock to face the claims of Christ, but [Havelock] was not particularly interested. Slowly, however, he saw that the Spirit of God, as he later wrote, was coming to him, 'with its offer of peace and mandate of love.' He consented to read, and Gardner lent him a life of Henry Martyn, the brilliant Cambridge don who had [laid down his life] in the East a dozen years before, preaching Christianity to Hindus and Mohammedans. He read a compendious volume of Christian evidences, compiled by a contemporary Northamptonshire parson. These and Gardner's own words, convinced him of his need.

Before the *General Kyd* reached Cape Town, therefore, 'love had prevailed.' Havelock had opened his life to Christ and, in his own words, a 'great change in his soul which has been productive of unspeakable advantage' had occurred. He was not slow to 'make public avowal' of his Christianity by seeking to live as he felt a Christian should, whilst Gardner and he regularly read the Bible and prayed together during the rest of the voyage. When Havelock reached Calcutta his determination to shine as a soldier had thus been linked to and absorbed by his determination to carry out the dictates of the Epistles to 'appear as lights in the world.'

August 1826 was hot and steamy in the Irrawaddy valley of Burma, where British forces, their scarlet uniforms contrasting with the dark jungle green, were pushing their way slowly against the brutal and well-trained troops of the king of Ava.

Henry Havelock had joined the army in the field after the fall of Rangoon. He had shown himself an efficient officer and stiff disciplinarian in his three years in India. He was, however, somewhat unpopular with his brother officers, being both too rigid in his morals and too abrupt in his comments for their liking. But the path he had taken was hard; though his men might appreciate his efforts to convert them, loose-living officers had little time for his ways. He was, therefore, lonely and often on edge. Such hardships merely spurred him on, though somewhat subduing his humour. But he knew already that spiritual warfare could be as rough as a soldier's battle.

In captured Rangoon he had continued the training of his men. He found also that no chaplain had been appointed. From this followed the experience of a brother officer, sightseeing in a Burmese pagoda, who was somewhat surprised to hear psalm singing in such an unexpected place. He tracked down the sound, entered an inner sanctum of the temple and found Havelock leading a group of soldiers in an informal service, while round the room were small stone Buddhas with oil lamps perched rakishly on their laps.

When eventually Havelock was sent up to the front the hot season was at its height. Enemy forays were increasing. Bodies of sentries caught unawares would be discovered shockingly mutilated. Sir Archibald Campbell the Commander-in-Chief, found his men jittery and occasionally out of hand, and matters were not improved by the appearance of three wild prophetesses in the Burmese ranks, whose frenzied screams heard at night through the jungle were too eerie for joking. Nights and days were harassing. It was then that an incident occurred, which became something of a legend in the Army: an outpost was set on at night and a runner came back to headquarters for instant support. Campbell sent an Orderly to the next company on the roster. The Orderly re-appeared with the company officer, who had to confess that half his men were drunk.

Campbell swore roundly and turned to his Aide-de-Camp. 'Then call out Havelock's saints,' he roared, 'they are always sober and can be depended on and Havelock himself is always ready.' In 1828 Henry Havelock, back from the war in Burma but still a Lieutenant, was Adjutant at the depot at Chinsura on the Hoogly not far from Calcutta.

He spent much of his leisure at Serampore, the nearby Baptist missionary settlement, presided over by the great William Carey, where one of his greatest friends, John Marshman, lived with his mother and youngest sister, nineteen-year-old Hannah Marshman, a gay young lady fresh from schooling in England. On June 14th Havelock wrote a long letter to Miss Hannah asking for her hand.

In reply he received a note, 'short and penned in a spirit of *very exemplary caution*,' but sufficient to give 'much encouragement and consolation.' Mrs Marshman also wrote encouragingly, but referred to his poverty and said she could not allow a definite engagement until Dr Marshman returned from Europe. Havelock thought this 'a little cruel' and wondered why John Marshman could not act on his father's behalf.

The following weekend Havelock was able to get down to Serampore and knew without a shadow of doubt that his love was fully returned and that whatever Dr Marshman might say the family looked on the two as engaged. 'I would not exchange for half the years which I have lived, the evening of Sunday last,' he wrote to Hannah when he had returned to his damp and lonely bungalow at Chinsura.

It is necessary that you should first have seen and felt all the calamity and vicissitude which I have witnessed; and been conversant as I have been with jealousy, calumny, strife, debate and turmoil before you comprehend as I did in that happy hour the joy of having peace and consolation and love spoken to me by one nurtured in the purest piety, and of feeling that the affection and fidelity which was then promised me was not that which could cease with time but such as would survive and continue to bless into eternity.

In 1829 they were married.

Two years later Havelock re-joined the 13th Light Infantry, bringing Hannah and their little boy, Harry, to Dinapore. Although his duties were slight, he was determined to be the best soldier in the Regiment, and for a definite purpose. 'It was,' he recalled in later years, 'the great object of my ambition to be surpassed by none in zeal and determination in the path of my duty because I was resolved to put down the vile calumny that a Christian could not be a meritorious soldier.'

With men living under the awful moral conditions typical of every British Regiment then in India, Havelock re-started his Bible meeting. A few survived of his earlier group, the chief being a Sergeant George Godfrey. Not unnaturally Godfrey and his fellows followed their leader into Baptist allegiance, and built a makeshift chapel.

The small group of thoroughgoing Christians met each morning and evening in their chapel for hymn singing, Bible reading and prayer. The building also provided an opportunity not otherwise allowed for in a military cantonment, of 'small places for retirement for private devotion, to which many resort,' as Havelock wrote to his father-in-law Dr Marshman.

On Sundays, after the men had attended the obligatory parade service, there is public worship before noon, and in the evening. I think [continued Havelock] the congregation on the latter occasion fluctuates between fifty and sixty, sometimes however exceeding this latter number; and it is admitted by those who, without any prepossession in favour of the faith, have the best opportunities of judging of the fact, that instances of immorality or neglect of duty among this body in the course of a year are very rare. The frequenters of this chapel are reckoned among the best behaved men in the Regiment.

And thus, in those days of the early 1830s at Dinapore, young Privates who had almost forgotten childhood attendance in an English country church, or who since earliest days in slum streets had never had the chance of hearing the Christian Gospel, would risk the ribaldry[28] of their friends and take a seat at the back of the chapel on a Sunday evening.

When the singing and prayers were done, Havelock preached. He knew what they needed, and could speak it in clipped, simple phrases: 'Time is short, and eternity at hand,' he would say, and the men remembered the dozen or more of their comrades buried in the past six or nine months, 'so I must not delay to speak to you on the most important of all subjects – the care and prospects of your immortal souls.'

When the service was over he would, if a man so desired, speak with him individually, showing from his Bible the way in which he might, 'have Jesus for [his] friend.' For those moments the relationship of officer and ranker was forgotten, to be resumed inexorably when they left the chapel.

All this was done, so Havelock wrote years later, 'in the very teeth of ridicule and opposition.'

One couple alone stood quietly for Havelock – Robert Sale, the commanding officer, and Florentia, his masterful and determined wife. Hannah gave all support in her power. 'I trust,' she wrote in August 1831, 'that my dear Henry will be spared to continue to use all his efforts to be useful to the soldiers, among whom he is greatly beloved.'

Late in 1834 the Adjutancy of the 13th, now at Agra, was vacant, and Havelock applied, without much hope of receiving the appointment.

Hannah was away at Serampore. One day she boldly wrote a letter to Lord William Bentinck the Governor-General and sent it across to Barrackpore. Shortly afterwards a red-and-gold-liveried servant called at the mission house with a request from Lord William that Hannah should do him the goodness to call. She stepped into the Governor-General's barge and was carried swiftly across the river to the fine park with its zoo and artificial hills.

Lady William Bentinck received her. Lord William entered, smiling and carrying a bundle of letters. 'About that letter you wrote me, madam,' he began, 'I am going to read you a few other letters I have received on the subject from your husband's Regiment.' Hannah was all of a flutter. Lord William then said, 'Before I allude to this correspondence I give you the assurance that I have bestowed the Adjutancy of the 13th on your husband because he is unquestionably the fittest man for it.'

Hannah subsided with relief, and Lord William began to read out from the letters. One called Havelock a Methodist and a fanatic. Another begged the Governor-General to realise that Havelock's, 'character as an officer was lowered by familiar intercourse with the men,' and a third respectfully intimated to his Lordship that strong religious views would destroy an Adjutant's impartiality.

Lord William said he had made enquiries and was convinced that Havelock's men were the most sober and well-disciplined in the Regiment. 'Give your husband my compliments and tell him he must continue his religious exertions, and if possible convert the whole Regiment. He can baptise the lot if he likes. But,' he added with a smile, tapping the letters, 'the *Adjutant* must not preach.'

Whatever the critics' disgust at Bentinck's choice, Havelock quickly won their loyalty and an inspecting General later in 1835 reported that 'the greatest unanimity seems to prevail among the officers of the Regiment.'

The work in the chapel continued, not without sacrifice, for Hannah who told her mother that 'Henry is at his office all the morning and I do enjoy his society so much when he comes home that I am quite jealous of the time he spends among the soldiers.' Hannah herself was busy teaching her own boys and putting in time among the children of the Regiment who[m] she found had no religious instruction in their school, and helping men of the chapel to learn to read.

In their home, each day began with family prayers, by no means yet common even in England, and on one such occasion an Irish servant, daughter of one of the men in the Regiment, provided a tale long current among the Havelocks. The Adjutant's extempore prayer had reduced the girl to tears and as she rose from her knees she blurted out, 'Oh Misther dear, you're not fit for a soldier. It's too tinderhearted you are. Sure you was born a praist, and a praist you ought to be.'

At the Regiment's next station, Kamal, Henry Havelock, now a Brevet-Captain, began a new work. Though he had won men to faith and character, he had failed to break the worst habit of the Regiment. The Divisional General at his last inspection in Agra had commented on the 'many courts marital which proceeded from habitual drunkenness... '

In the garrison Havelock met an old friend, Edward Wakefield of a Native Regiment. They discussed this problem together and Wakefield mentioned an abortive attempt in a battalion of the Buffs at Fort William in 1833 to form a Temperance Society, a British and Foreign Temperance Society having recently been formed in England. The idea struck Havelock as he passed it to Sale, remarking, 'We've tried everything else.' Sale approved and a Regimental Temperance Association was formed, of men pledged to abjure alcohol. But to expect them to honour such a surprising and original pledge was impossible unless a counter attraction was provided. Sale therefore secured the Commander-in-Chief's permission to allocate £90 from the Canteen Fund for the building of a Coffee Room, such as had never been seen in an Indian cantonment.

When it was built, Sergeant Godfrey, who was advanced in years, was placed in charge. 'We put him at the bar of the Coffee Room,' recalled Wakefield, 'his wife made the coffee and he distributed it. We gave them [the men] a cup of good coffee for about three farthings. We gave them the *Penny Magazine* and other papers to read, and we had meetings.' 'By pure moral persuasion,' as Wakefield put it, the 13th soon had strong membership for their Regimental Temperance Association. Within a few months General Duncan officially reported its strength at 'two-hundred-and-seventy-four persons.' 'Havelock's crotchet,' as the men called the Temperance drive, had caught on.

The scheme gradually expanded. A Savings Bank was established. 'Mrs Sale joined in and we had our monthly meetings for the wives of the men and their children, and we gave them buns and cakes, and they enjoyed themselves.' Havelock wrote to Adjutants of other British Regiments in India, and in the course of the next two years some thirty units formed Temperance Societies; reports from them were read out at monthly meetings in the 13th. By June 1838, when General Duncan again inspected the Regiment, he reported a definite improvement. 'Courts martial continue to be numerous, but they appear all to be held on the same set of men for habitual drunkenness.'

In January 1842 the British garrison of Jalalabad, a small fortress town beyond the Khyber Pass, realised that they were isolated. A few days before, they had been shocked by the arrival of a solitary horseman, unarmed, wounded and exhausted, the sole survivor of the garrison of the Afghan capital, Kabul. Dr Brydon's arrival and the three hopeless days of beacon-lights and bugle-calls that followed had convinced General Sale and his command that the whole British force, which an unwise Government had risked in a futile attempt to occupy Afghanistan, had been wiped out by treachery in the Khurd–Kabul pass.

Siege was inevitable. Far to the east a relieving force was slowly pushing its way through mountainous and hostile country. The question was whether famine and the Afghan Army would combine to eliminate Jalalabad before General Pollock could arrive to relieve it. The garrison was merely an under-strength brigade. They had six weeks' provisions.

Havelock, now a full captain but nothing more, was attached to the staff of his former Colonel. When the trouble with Persia and Afghanistan had broken out in 1838, Sale had left to a command and Havelock to be Persian interpreter to General Elphinstone, the martyr to gout in whose incapable hands the expedition had been placed. During the next two years of battles, shady diplomacy and uneasy occupation, Havelock had his fill of excitement. By the time the British envoy had been murdered and Elphinstone, his gout now excruciating, had sealed the fate of his troops by capitulation, Havelock had re-joined Sale and thus was in Jalalabad.

The arrival of Dr Brydon, [sole] 'remnant of an army,' threw the British garrison into gloom.

The whole force was awed and shaken by the proximity of a disaster unparalleled in British Indian history. The next Sunday Havelock, who had maintained his informal Bible meetings with such men as were off duty, suggested a partial cessation of work in order that divine service might be held. Sale invited him to read the service.

The European officers and men assembled in a square of Bala Hissar, with the Union Jack fluttering overhead from the tower.

> *Everyone came as usual, with sword and pistol or musket and bayonet, [wrote one officer], and with sixty rounds in pouch, ready at a moment's notice to march to battle. To me it was an affecting sight to see those great rough fellows of the 13th, with their heads bowed, humbly confessing their sins before God, and acknowledging their dependence on His goodness and mercy.*

The familiar Church of England morning service sounded moving and impressive as Havelock read, in his clear, rather abrupt voice. For the Psalm of the day he substituted Psalm 46, 'which,' he remarked, 'Luther was wont to use in seasons of peculiar difficulty and depression; and the men all joined in the words of it: "God is our refuge and strength, a very present help in trouble..."'

In that spirit they fought the siege, which began a fortnight later on 15th February 1842. An untimely earthquake nearly put an end to their efforts, and by mid-March famine was 'staring us in the face.' A courageous little sortie from the walls, however, seized a convenient flock of sheep and saved the situation. The rank and file were admirable and Havelock gleefully and accurately ascribed their morale to the convenient loss of the rum supply some months earlier. The weeks passed, and the relieving force under General Sir George Pollock[29] seemed as far away as ever. Then came a report that Pollock had been defeated. Havelock urged Sale to attack.

Early in the morning of 7th April Akbar Khan, the Afghan general, who was preparing for final victory, found himself vigorously attacked instead. A few days earlier Havelock had written, 'I am relying fully on the merits of the Redeemer and will be well pleased, if it be His will, to end my days in so honourable an enterprise;' and in the melee he was thrown from his horse and nearly killed. But by the time the sun was fully up Akbar's camp was in ashes and his army in flight. Four of Elphinstone's guns were back in British hands, much plunder had been taken, and the siege effectually raised.

The honours of the day, as no one doubted or grudged, were with Havelock. And to the end of his life he kept the anniversary of this 'crowning mercy.'

Nine days afterwards Pollock's relieving army, which had not been defeated, marched into Jalalabad (under whose walls they had expected a famous victory) while the garrison band played 'Oh! But ye've been long o'coming.'

Ten years later, in 1852, Lieutenant Colonel Havelock, CB had arrived back in India after two years' leave in England — his first for twenty-six years. He had held staff appointments and had taken part in the various minor wars of the later forties, but promotion was dishearteningly slow. Although Lord Hardinge could call him 'every inch a soldier and every inch a Christian' he could not take 'the path of popularity, the broad way... Principles alone are worth living for.' Thus, as he wrote at the age of fifty-nine, he 'could not hope to be a Major-General before seventy-one.'

He was so poor that the education of his family worried him. He found himself, to his own disgust, touting for influence and recommendations. 'How can I help it? I have soldiered with heart and *soul* for thirty-nine years and my country's generals neglect me.' But he did not waver in his faith. His philosophy is neatly expressed in a letter to his small son: 'Take care that you have Jesus for your friend... be a credit to your name and country.' His spiritual life was no longer so lonely, for his own quiet efforts had combined with the changing atmosphere in England to increase the number of wholehearted Christians in the Indian civil and military services. Thus Sir John and Sir Henry Lawrence, John Nicholson and James Outram, all famous names of the period, were strong Christians; and so were many others.

But the unkindest cut of all, in his return to India, was the need to leave his wife in England for the children's sake. 'If you knew what I endured since I parted from you... ' he wrote on the way back, 'but my God will support me: I have Jesus Christ to trust and His presence to comfort me.' The early fifties were lean years for Havelock. But, though he did not know it, his day was coming.

June 1857 in Calcutta. The general consternation at the Sepoy mutiny, which had burst out at Meerut in early May and was now blazing throughout the Bengal army, had been absorbed by the general preparations for its suppression. The Governor-General, Canning, refused to realise the gravity of the position; the Commander-in-Chief had most inconveniently died; India was denuded of troops, for a war with Persia was only just over; an army must be raised to besiege Delhi, but a mobile column, it was thought, was enough for the mutineers in Oudh.

Havelock, full Colonel and acting Brigadier-General, was on his way back from Persia, where he had distinguished himself. Before the Battle of Mohumra he had written to his wife, 'I have good troops and cannon, but my trust is in the Lord Jesus, my tried and merciful friend.' After the victory he wrote again, 'the cannonade was warm... I felt throughout that the Lord Jesus was at my side.' And now the new Commander-in-Chief appointed him to command the mobile column.

Havelock was obscure, 'an old fossil, dug up and only fit to be turned into pipe-clay.' He was, 'not in fashion,' as Lady Canning wrote, 'but all the same we believe he will do well. No doubt he is fussy and tiresome,' she added, 'but his little old stiff figure looks as active and fit for use as if he were made of steel.'

On 24th June 1857 he took command at Allahabad. There followed two months of splendid, impossible victories which made Havelock's name a household word in India and England. His force was absurdly small, and the heat was intense, yet an inefficient Government had left his Highlanders to fight in winter woollen uniforms. The one advantage he had was the new Enfield rifle.

The first task was to recapture Cawnpore and rescue the women and children prisoners. His little column trounced the rebels at Fatehpur and Havelock wrote home, 'One of the prayers oft repeated throughout my life has been answered, and I have lived to command in a successful action.' His Order of the Day attributed the victory to 'the Enfield rifle... British pluck... and the blessing of Almighty God.' The last phrase was unusual for the times, but Havelock had deliberately chosen it.

Just short of Cawnpore his force was on the verge of defeat, held up by heavy gunfire which caused one Regiment to waver. As Henry Havelock, the General's eldest son, described the moment of danger, in a letter home:

> It was the turning point of the day and of our campaign. If we had receded one inch not a hundred of us would ever have got back to the shelter of the walls of Allahabad. I must confess that I felt absolutely sick with apprehension, and if I looked calm, I never was before and hope never to be again in such a funk in my life. The enemy thought we were lying down from fear.
>
> Just then the dear old Governor rode bareheaded to the front,

spoke half a dozen words — and at the magic of his example up sprang the line, and advanced. And that advance saved India.

Havelock had seen the waver. He had sent an urgent message to the guns but realised he could not wait. He rode round, Harry said, to the front of the prostrate Highlanders, calmly smiling while bullets and shells whizzed and whined within an inch of his face.

With increasing darkness the shadows lengthened, [wrote Major North], which added to the imposing effect of the rebel line. General Havelock, who had just had his horse shot under him, now appeared boldly riding a hack, the only man who dared raise his head — so close and thick was the fire that rained upon us.

He reined up with his back to the fire, facing the line, and spoke clearly, firmly and without a trace of excitement, and still smiling: 'the longer you look at it, men, the less you will like it. Rise up. The brigade will advance, left battalion leading.'

Hardly were the words spoken, [wrote North], when a feeling of confidence inspired every breast and displaced the overwhelming weight and uncertainty and doubt engendered by inaction. Up sprang our thinned line... the odds being fearfully against us. But to this act of intrepidity in our General his troops worthily responded.

In the action which followed, Harry himself won the Victoria Cross by an act of incredible bravery.

On 17th July Havelock entered Cawnpore too late. Nana Sahib, the rebel leader, had massacred his prisoners and thrown their bodies down a well. When Havelock's soldiers found the well and the blood-stained room of butchery, they were maddened. Only his firmness prevented a ghastly revenge on the Cawnpore inhabitants. He promptly bought up all looted wines and spirits. Otherwise, 'I should scarcely have a sober soldier in camp;' there had been drunkenness enough already.

He forced the Ganges and pressed on towards besieged Lucknow. His fifteen-hundred men fought four more battles against overwhelming odds. 'I have fought seven fights with the enemy and by God's blessing have beat him in every one. But,' he added, 'things are in a most perilous state.' Every casualty mattered, for he had no reserves, they were in hostile country and Lucknow's need was pressing. On 31st July, to the Lucknow garrison's despair, the victorious Havelock was forced to retire and await reinforcements. His column had no more than a thousand men still fit, and even they looked 'ragged, woebegone, bearded ruffians.' Havelock shared every hardship and often slept on the ground with his horse saddled beside him. His column, with Lucknow, was being sacrificed on the altar of Government ineptitude.

In September, back at Cawnpore, he was joined by fresh troops under Outram, his senior officer. With memorable chivalry Outram waived his rights of command, to give Havelock the glory of relieving Lucknow. This action was splendid but unwise, for Outram continued to advise (and expected to be listened to), sometimes against Havelock's better judgment.

They pressed on together. At the end of September they fought their way into the besieged Lucknow residency, after violent battles. 'Rarely has a commander,' wrote the Governor-General in a General Order, 'been so fortunate as to relieve by his success as many aching hearts, or to reap so rich a reward of gratitude as will deservingly be offered to Brigadier General Havelock and his gallant band, wherever their triumph shall be known.'

His force was too weak either to withdraw the garrison or drive off the enemy. But though the siege continued, his action and earlier victories, his personal courage and the endurance of his troops had made his name a household word.

He was promoted Major General and knighted. His wife at home found herself suddenly launched into high society. Not least, Victorian England revelled in the glamour of the 'old puritan soldier,' 'that preaching, praying, psalm singing man,' a latter-day Cromwell or Hampden. At sixty-three Havelock had come into his own.

He never lived to enjoy his glory. For nearly two months Havelock and Outram held on in Lucknow. In November Sir Colin Campbell arrived with a strong force to relieve them. The garrison broke out to join him, and while the battle was still raging the three Generals met on the outskirts. Havelock, although already ill, had run twenty-five yards under fire to greet Campbell. A week later, worn out by his efforts and struck down by dysentery, he died, 'happy and contented,' in a common soldier's tent, not knowing that the news of his death would throw Britain into national mourning, and greatly advance many of the religious and reforming causes he had pioneered.

In Lucknow, the night before he died, he lay in his one faded uniform. He scarcely slept though suffering little, and his mind was clear. When the thirst was bad he would call and Harry would bring him water, his father smiling weakly, abundantly happy that they were one in heart and spirit. Daylight came. Havelock called faintly, 'Harry, Harry.' As Harry answered, Havelock looked up, smiling. 'Harry,' he said, 'see how a Christian can die.'

9

Lieutenant General Sir Arthur Smith

KCB KBE DSO MC LLD

'…the simplicity that is in Christ'

By Brigadier WIC Dobbie

It was Lord Hardinge who said of General Havelock, the devoted Christian officer who was to become famous for his part in the relief of Lucknow, that he was 'every inch a Christian and every inch a soldier.' This description would be equally appropriate of Lieutenant General Sir Arthur Smith, who died on 8th August 1977, leaving behind him an inspiring and abiding influence both as an officer and as a Christian.

Arthur Francis Smith was born on 9th December 1890. His ancestors had been bankers in Nottingham but his father, Colonel Granville Smith, served with distinction in the Coldstream Guards and brought his family up in Derbyshire. This was a loving, Christian home and Arthur Smith could never recall a day when he did not trust Christ, and Christ alone, for salvation. He was always grateful for this and, when in his later years he was asked publicly what was the best age to start presenting Christian truth to children, it is not surprising that he recommended parents 'to start at the age of nought!'

His boyhood was a happy and successful one. He had a quick, clear mind and was gifted physically. He won the school quarter-mile and half-mile events at athletics, rowed for the Eton 1st VIII, and was a gifted horseman. He took naturally to soldiering and was commissioned from Sandhurst into his father's regiment in 1910, after being awarded the Sword of Honour. From his earliest years it was evident that his parents' prayers had been answered and that God's sovereign hand directed his young life.

World War One and Marriage

The beginning of Arthur Smith's commissioned service was spent in England and Egypt. Besides maintaining his sporting interests, he ran Bible studies for his soldiers and his soldierly acumen was so obvious that early in World War One he became Adjutant of the 3rd Battalion, the Coldstream Guards. It is said that, although he spent the latter part of the war on the staff, his heart was really in the trenches. He was mentioned in dispatches five times and was awarded the DSO, the MC and French Croix de Guerre. (He confided to his family that he dreaded attending the investiture for the foreign decoration as he would have to tolerate being kissed by a Frenchman on both cheeks!)

This war not only brought Arthur Smith honours and awards; it brought him wounds also. No less than three times he had to be carried out of action.

At the outbreak of war his father gave him a small Bible. Written on the flyleaf were the verses 'For you have made the Lord... your dwelling place. No evil will befall you... For He will give His angels charge concerning you, to guard you in all your ways.'[30]

His father recommended that Arthur Smith always carry the Bible in his pocket, as he himself had done whilst serving in the South African War. Taking this practical advice to heart, Arthur Smith had a pocket tailored into his trousers for this very purpose! Two experiences illustrated the absolute truth of this Scripture to him.

In November 1914, whilst Smith was reconnoitering a route in the middle of the night, a German shell burst very close, quickly followed by another that caught him on the hip and hurled him across the road.

As he lay wounded at the dressing station en route to hospital, he wondered why it was that a shell that could hurl him across a road, had not done more damage. When he pulled out his Bible, he discovered that it had caught the main force of the shrapnel and had diverted it from its course so that, instead of being wounded very seriously, he had only received a flesh wound.

It was only when he finally reached a hospital that he discovered that the shrapnel had cut through his Bible as far as, and had stopped exactly at, Psalm 91, the Psalm of his father's choosing.

In August 1917, whilst on the staff of XIV Corps, Arthur Smith and two other staff officers were sent to Langemarck to carry out a reconnaissance. Approaching the trenches furthest forward, they were caught in a German artillery bombardment.

There was a terrific bang, something seemed to kick his leg, and he found himself knocked to the ground by the explosion. As

Lt Gen Sir Arthur Smith's damaged Bible, open at Psalm 91.

his companions picked themselves up, Arthur Smith found himself unable to do so. Looking down at his leg he saw his foot swinging about, seemingly attached by little more than his puttee,[31] with quite a respectable portion of his leg missing completely.

At the dressing station, aptly named Mendingem, Arthur Smith's final instruction to the surgeon was 'Don't take that foot off, doctor; give it a chance.' On waking from the anaesthetic, he was relieved to find he was still in possession of his left foot! A couple of days later at the General Hospital at Rouen, the surgeon examined him and said 'I can leave your foot on, on chance; but you may get blood-poisoning with fatal results: or I can amputate and you will get on all right. Let me know tomorrow morning what you feel about it.'

This ultimatum did not disturb Arthur Smith, as he thought on the words of the Bible, 'And we know that God causes all things to work together for good to those who love God, to those who are called according to His purpose.'[32] Later that day he took his *Daily Light*, a book of Bible verses for each day of the year, and opened it to that day's reading (19th October). He was staggered when the first words he read were 'The Lord shall be thy confidence, and shall keep thy foot from being taken.'[33] That was sufficient encouragement and, thanking God, he closed the book. He kept his foot, was passed as fully fit in 1925, and in his own words, 'wobbled my way in the Army till I retired in 1948.' Arthur Smith was to find that the Lord has an amazing way of turning disappointment into victory. While he was recovering from his wounds in a nursing home in Park Lane he met Monica Crossley, who was acting as a ward maid. He invited her to his home, where for the first time she heard and saw at first hand the power of true Christianity. She was to say, years later, that at the end of a weekend in that home, like the blind man healed by Christ, 'whereas I was blind, now I could see.'

Arthur Smith and Monica Crossley were married in 1918. Their home was to be the source of lasting happiness not only to their children but also to scores of others who visited it. Shortly before Smith's death, a young Guards officer described the Arthur Smiths as the happiest married couple he knew and in the closing years of their married life together their contemporaries described them as 'love-birds!'

Arthur Smith was as strict a disciplinarian in his home as he was professionally, but his children loved both their parents and all of them inherited their Christian faith in due season.

Between the Wars

After the Armistice, Arthur Smith was sent to the Staff College at Camberley, as it was felt that he could continue to convalesce and study at the same time. As a student, he ran a weekly lunchtime Bible study group for his brother officers. Over two decades later a fellow student, who had by then become Commander-in-Chief, remarked that he regretted not having attended that Bible study group as it would have taught him principles he would have valued later.

From 1921 to 1924, Arthur Smith was Adjutant at Sandhurst. His briskness and efficiency were legendary and he achieved the high standards that were rightly demanded. It was during this tour that he compiled *100 Days* – a booklet of 100 Bible studies on selected subjects. This was born out of a realisation of a need for a book to help Gentlemen Cadets to understand the Bible. The comments may seem slightly dated or even 'Prussian' to a modern reader, but they are memorable, apposite even in various languages, and in 1976 new editions were published in America, Belgium, and Turkey. The worldwide use of this booklet over 50 years reveals that it was a labour born and blessed of God and a remarkable achievement by a layman in his early thirties who had been through an exacting war.

The two decades between the wars were possibly the years in which Arthur Smith's personal Christian influence was greatest. Many who came under his influence at Sandhurst and during the tours that followed (such as Commandant of the Guards Depot, Commanding Officer of the 2nd Battalion, The Coldstream Guards and Commander, 4th Guards Brigade) remained lifelong friends. Throughout his life, his loyalty to all with whom he came into contact was outstanding. Widows of brother officers killed in the First World War were visited regularly, relations in difficult circumstances were cared for, and charities generously supported. He was unusually far-seeing in his practical Christianity for a man of his time.

While in command at Caterham he saw the inadequacy of quarters for Non-Commissioned Officers and guardsmen and consequently inspired and oversaw the building of 32 married quarters. They called him 'Salvation Arthur' and 'Padre Smith'! These nicknames amused him and reflected the respect and affection with which his brother officers and soldiers regarded him. They knew that behind his brisk exterior was a shy man with an intensely kind heart and an unaffectedly sincere interest in their welfare.

It was during this tour that a member of the garrison church choir asked him for a recommendation to become a missionary. Arthur Smith asked him whether he had a message. It appeared he had not. Years later the two men ran into each other again in Oxford and the enquirer stated that he now had a true experience of Christ in his life, that he now had a real message, had been ordained, and that he used *100 Days* to inspire his sermons! The direct question asked years before had set off a chain of events, which led to this man's conversion.

Arthur Smith never sought to hold centre-stage. He used to say that he only got promoted because he never had to pass an examination! He knew well that selfish ambition was proscribed by God (Jeremiah 45:5) and abhorred it; but he had honoured God, and now God honoured him (1 Samuel 2:30).

The Second World War

From 1938 onwards, he held a number of key senior-staff appointments over a period of four years. While commanding 4th Guards Brigade, Wavell had been his Divisional Commander and when Wavell took over Middle East Command, Arthur Smith was retained as his Chief of Staff. John Connell, in his biographies of both Wavell and his successor Auchinleck, informs us that Arthur Smith had a deep admiration and affection for both of them. This affection was mutual.

Wavell described Arthur Smith as 'a very fine character indeed, a charming personality and an excellent staff officer... very conscientious and accurate, had a delightful sense of humour, was the very soul of honour and uprightness, organised a staff well and ran an extremely happy show.' Smith modestly informed Connell that he found such praise from a man like Wavell very humbling and added, 'I may be permitted to say that I often wondered why he was apparently satisfied with me as Chief of Staff. I really did, for I had no originality and disliked tanks and aeroplanes and all the mechanical things of modern warfare.'

His relationship with Auchinleck was no less warm than that with his predecessor. His steadiness and loyalty to both Commanders-in-Chief were invaluable throughout the vicissitudes of the Desert Campaign. On two occasions Arthur Smith was offered command of a Corps, once by Churchill himself. It says much of his humility that he declined such an appointment, giving the reason that he had not had experience of commanding a formation in modern warfare.

The next two years were spent as General Officer Commanding London District with as many as 250,000 men under command at one time, but in 1944 he was appointed Commander-in-Chief Persia and Iraq Command. The Chief of the Imperial General Staff was Alanbrooke and he asked to see Arthur Smith before he left. In his diary that night Alanbrooke wrote: 'Finally Arthur Smith to say goodbye before departure for Iraq and Persia Command. There is no doubt that he is a very fine man, entirely selfless and with only one thought – that of serving his country.'

In this appointment, Arthur Smith had the responsibility of maintaining a supply line through Persia by which over 5 million tons of war material was delivered to Russia. He had always had exceptional ability in dealing with people and this gift was to be of paramount importance in maintaining the morale of his troops in a command that appeared to be a military backwater as well as in securing wise relationships with local tribesmen.

In October 1945 Arthur Smith was moved to India, where he filled a series of appointments over the next three years in the period leading up to Partition, ending up as Commander of British troops in India and Pakistan after Auchinleck's departure. These years were filled with fearful problems as power was transferred and his courtesy and impartiality, which did not always make him popular with politicians, must have been severely tried.

Retirement

When in 1948 Arthur Smith retired from the Army he gave himself unselfishly to numerous Christian charities and missions. He became Chairman of the Management Committee of Dr Barnardo's Homes, of the Officers' Christian Union, of the Soldiers' and Airmen's Scripture Readers Association, and of the Africa Inland Mission. He took part in the affairs of the Crusaders' Union, Kingham School, the Evangelical Alliance, and Miss Daniell's Soldiers' Home.

As a speaker, he was in regular demand. His style was simple. He sought 'clarity not cleverness, utterance not eloquence.' He made ample use of alliteration to help his hearers retain his message. There were those who felt he gave the impression of despising scholarship, but this conclusion was not fair. Arthur Smith emphasised the simplicity of the Gospel because he knew so well that many rejected the claims of Jesus Christ, not on intellectual grounds, but because of the moral implications.

In 1953, his only son, serving in the Coldstream Guards, was killed in an accident on holiday. No engagement was cancelled nor any letter of sympathy left unanswered and the funeral reflected the joyful triumph that Geoffrey was 'with Christ, for that is very much better.'[34]

At their golden wedding some years later, he and his wife asked their relations not to give them presents but, if they so wished, to make donations to Christian missions in which the couple took a particular interest.

Arthur Smith had transparent goodness of heart. He loathed advertisement, exhibitionism, and pomposity. He loved simplicity and his crisp sense of humour made him the subject of many amusing anecdotes. Unfortunately, some of the best of these are apocryphal, including the occasion when, on seeing so much unconventional dress in the desert, he is supposed to have issued the order 'If shorts are worn any shorter, they will be worn no longer!'

In his later years he found himself having to contend publicly for truth. He detested disputes but, when attempts were made even by the ecclesiastical hierarchy to pursue courses of action that he believed to be dishonouring God, he reluctantly felt bound to oppose them.

As he entered the evening of life he sought to pass on his responsibilities to younger men. Fortunately, he was persuaded in January 1977 to speak at Sandhurst. The occasion was memorable.

'You can tell your father,' he remarked as he left to the Commandant's daughter, with a twinkle, 'that I have been in his Academy for two hours, and so far I have heard nothing against him!'

'I only speak publicly once a year now,' he began, 'and that is in Strangeways Prison, Manchester. But it occurred to me that the Gospel which prisoners in Strangeways Prison require is precisely the same as required by cadets at Sandhurst!' The simplicity, the flair, the challenge, and the adventure of his Christian experience were still there. Shortly after that talk, one cadet put his trust in Jesus Christ and it seemed a mark of God's blessing that he was destined for Arthur Smith's own regiment, the Coldstream Guards. Smith was delighted, but insisted that the glory should be God's alone.

It is appropriate that this chapter should close with an anecdote. The scene is the 1976 Annual Meeting of the Soldiers' and Airmen's Scripture Readers Association. It is traditional that at the evening meeting a number of servicemen in uniform, one by one, go up to a microphone, state their name, and give a brief testimony of how God has blessed them. The chairman at this meeting, as it drew to a close, suggested that General Sir Arthur Smith might like to give a word of testimony. We can picture, in our mind's eye, the way the General would have limped over to the microphone (for his wounds had left their mark). We can imagine him breathing up a small prayer that he would be given something to say that would honour his Master and be helpful to his hearers. We can imagine a hushed expectancy.

'My name is Smith!' he began (peals of laughter), 'and it is my testimony,' he added with conviction, 'that God saves and God keeps.' He sat down. It was so simple and typical of the man who had endeavoured to 'please the one who enlisted him as a soldier.'[35]

10

William Dobbie

Defender of Malta

By Don Stephens

Defend Malta at all costs.' This was no easy order for any British commanding officer in early 1940. It filled General William Dobbie's mind as his plane landed on the island in the early hours of Sunday, 28th April. The new governor and Commander-in-Chief was sixty, recently retired with forty years' service behind him. He was about to face the severest challenge of his life.

Within weeks of his arrival, Hitler became master of Western Europe. When his fascist ally, Mussolini, dictator of Italy, joined him in making war on Britain, they formed a genuine axis of evil.

Malta is a little island in the Mediterranean Sea, seventeen miles long and nine miles at its widest. It is like an unsinkable 'aircraft carrier' anchored sixty miles away from Italian territory. From it the British had the potential to ruin the enemy's supply route and its 'Grand Plan,' which was to be an attempt to seize North Africa as a hopeful prelude to pushing east through Egypt to southern Russia and its oil. It was all part of the dream of worldwide conquest.

Two years later, after furious fighting that involved an average of three immense air raids a day, Malta remained bloody but unbowed, in spite of literally being 'the most bombed place on the earth.'

One officer who watched Dobbie while bombs were falling all around him remarked, 'He paid no more attention to them than to rain.'

Another man who served alongside him later made a BBC broadcast in which he described him as 'a big man – big physically, big professionally, and big morally.'

Francis Gerard also knew him at first hand during the siege. In his book *Malta Magnificent*, he comments on Dobbie's 'complete fearlessness' amidst the crash and choking dust of the bombs.

Perceptively, Churchill wrote of William Dobbie that he was 'a Governor of outstanding character who inspired all ranks and classes, military and civil, with his determination; a Cromwellian figure at the key point... fighting with his Bible in one hand and his sword in the other.'

Dobbie found his way into the history books for leading the British response to Italian and German aggression on Malta, but the rest of his career has largely been overlooked.

Before William was born in India in 1879, the Dobbie family had long been committed Christians. His father was in the Indian Civil Service and other relatives served in the army. The Christian faith would be a marked feature of the life of William Dobbie. As a Christian he 'practised the presence of God.' No matter what the circumstances, he prayed. His writings are filled with references to his faith and the nearness of God.

He had a conversion experience while at Charterhouse School. On the first Sunday in November 1893, when he was fourteen, he felt 'that things were not right between God and me and that I was unfit to stand in his sight.' Dobbie felt his unworthiness when confronted by the holiness of God. This sense of inadequacy became a spiritual burden. Later, summing up his feelings, he recorded: 'My need of a Saviour was brought home to me.'

William Dobbie wrote that

> *Jesus Christ, the Son of God, came into this world for the express purpose of giving His life so that He might bear, and pay the penalty of my sin so that I might go free. That night I accepted the Lord Jesus as my Saviour, my Companion, and my God – just by myself – there was nobody else in the room. That was the turning point of my life. The past, bad though it was in God's sight, was blotted out; Christ's presence and help were promised for the present, and the future was assured. I thank God more than I can say for that wonderful event in November 1893.*

What Dobbie describes is a typical sudden evangelical conversion. Saul on the Damascus road is a biblical example of this. Dobbie did not doubt that an authentic personal relationship with God had been formed. There were no second thoughts. He was baptised as a believer and attached himself to what would now be called an 'Open Brethren' evangelical church.

He took the usual Christian view that there is meaning to life as a whole and therefore that God must have a plan for his life. Charterhouse School had entered him for the examination to enter the Royal Military Academy, Woolwich. He passed. Though there was a pacifist tradition in his church, he accepted the open door into the academy as God's plan that he should become a soldier.

It was 1897. Dobbie was six feet three inches (1.90 metres) tall, solidly built, athletic and clever. Two years later he was commissioned as a second lieutenant in the Royal Engineers. He was a sapper, a military engineer.

His first public military duty was to be part of the guard at Queen Victoria's funeral in 1901. Smart in full-dress scarlet uniform, he stood by the park railings at Piccadilly. Soon afterwards he was plunged into the middle of the Boer War. Interestingly, he later took the view that this was an unjust war.

In 1904, again in full-dress uniform, he married Sybil. They had three children, one of whom was subsequently killed fighting the Nazis in Italy in 1944.

After various overseas postings, he decided to take the entrance examinations for the British Army's Staff College at Camberley. He was top of the fifty successful men in 1911. His graduation coincided with the outbreak of World War One in 1914.

World War One

Dobbie endured the horrors of that war, starting as a Captain and ending as a Lieutenant Colonel. When the British regulars came up against the Germans at Mons in 1914, it was numbers that overwhelmed them, not greater bravery or skill. Dobbie played a full part in the retreat from Mons. In 1915 shrapnel smashed the binoculars round his neck. On Christmas Day that year he walked along seventeen miles of British trenches in eight and a half hours with the aim of lifting the morale of the British troops.

He did not talk much about his work and what he had suffered. People often asked him what he did in the war. The usual laconic answer was: 'I ended it.' By that he meant that he was the officer on duty at British General Headquarters when news of the armistice was received. Dobbie dictated a telegram intended for every British soldier:

Hostilities will cease at 11.00 hours today. Troops will stand fast at the line reached at that hour. There will be no fraternisation with the enemy.

Signed: WGS Dobbie. Lieutenant Colonel, General Staff.
11th November 1918.

When personal letters to his wife became available, they showed in more detail how he reacted when surrounded by death and destruction on a vast scale. By nature, she was prone to worry. In contrast, he always looked on the bright side of life. Frequently he tells her after a battle: 'Our men were absolutely magnificent.' He took the same view of the enemy soldiers: 'The Germans opposite us are a fine lot and fought magnificently.' Sybil had doubts that he would survive the war, given the high casualty rate. Nor was she convinced that victory was possible. Dobbie tried to alter her perceptions. One letter gives her spiritual advice: 'Please don't try and bear the burden of things when the Lord wants to bear the burden for you.' Nobody who has any idea of the extent of the slaughter in the 1914–1918 war would have disagreed with Dobbie's sentiment when he wrote, 'Please God, this fighting will shorten the war.'

Some men blamed God for the war; Dobbie blamed the sin embedded in the heart of every man. Some lost whatever 'faith' they had; by contrast, Dobbie emerged from the carnage and misery as a Christian soldier who had grown closer to, and more dependent on, God. There were other soldiers like him with strong views about being a Christian believer in the midst of killing and terror. Brave chaplains and stretcher-bearers are examples, in addition to the men who did the fighting and dying. He mentions joining the Soldiers' Christian Association [SCA] (now the Soldiers' and Airmen's Scripture Readers' Association or SASRA). This included men of all ranks who met together to encourage one another. Sybil was told that the SCA 'have got a large room at Etaples where they hold meetings nightly with hundreds present.' His letters always reveal a man who did not just ask for God's help; he genuinely experienced God's nearness on a daily basis.

One incident in March 1918 made a big impression on him. Because Russia had made peace as a result of the Bolshevik Revolution of 1917, the German army was no longer fighting in the east. So all its resources could be aimed solely at the British and French in the west. At the time Dobbie was serving on the staff of the British Commander-in-Chief, Douglas Haig. The German army was on the verge of pushing the French and British armies apart.

At the end of March it became necessary to move a particular British division from the north to prevent a total breakthrough. If the Germans succeeded they would win the war. Dobbie knew all this. He telephoned for railway carriages to transport the men of the division immediately. The officer in charge of the rail links replied that it was impossible. No amount of argument or using higher rank worked. Dobbie records that he prayed, 'Lord, I have come to the end of my tether. It seems necessary to have that division if we are not to lose the war. Please help.'

Shortly afterwards the telephone rang. The rolling stock had unexpectedly become available. The division plugged the hole the Germans were punching in the defensive line.

In his book *A Very Present Help* Dobbie admits that this story raises many problems. For instance, it appears to suggest that God takes sides. It could have been a coincidence that railway vehicles became available when they did. What if a German was praying the opposite? But, whatever happened, he continued, 'I had no doubt in my mind that God intervened.' After all, he reasoned, the Bible is filled with stories of answered prayer. Furthermore, in Bible stories about war, God is often said to take sides.

On 4th August 1918 the British called an official day of prayer that was more widely observed than had been expected. British troops assembled near Amiens for a huge counter-attack. Surprise would save lives on both sides. It was physically impossible to conceal so many units. But suddenly the weather prevented German aircraft from flying over and seeing what was going on. Four days after the day of prayer the Battle of Amiens began, a hundred days of victories that led to the final German defeat. General Ludendorff, the German chief of staff, called this moment 'the black day of the German army.'

Interestingly, the next national day of prayer was held on 26th May 1940, though the decision pre-dated that Sunday. Dobbie's son was one of the helpless British soldiers hoping to be brought home from Dunkirk. In his desperation at the possible capture of the British army, King George VI called for a national day of prayer. Churchill's government supported him. Shortly after this, the English Channel went calm, so allowing boats an easy crossing to save the men stranded on Dunkirk's beaches. Even more remarkably, Hitler stopped his tank units from attacking. Historians still argue why he did it. The fact remains that this decision saved the army. Almost all the men were rescued. Churchill called it 'a great deliverance.'

William Dobbie contributed his piece to the mosaic of victory. As a result of his work in the First World War he was awarded the Distinguished Service Order (DSO). Six times the big, blond Dobbie was 'mentioned in dispatches' for 'gallant and distinguished services on the battlefield.' Also, the French gave him military honours, the Croix de Guerre and the Légion d'Honneur. So did the Belgians.

Interwar Years

In 1929 Dobbie was in charge of operations during the Palestine Emergency. The League of Nations, formed after the First World War, gave Britain the task, or mandate, to rule Palestine. Tensions between Jews and Arabs emerged almost immediately.

Based at Jerusalem, Dobbie had too few British troops available to keep the peace. The town of Gaza was in the path of several thousand armed Bedouin known to be intent on murder and looting. A British mission hospital was a target for these men, who were inflamed by propaganda and hate. Dobbie wrote, 'In my need I asked for God's special help and intervention. I knelt down and told him that I was at the end of my resources.' For a while the Arabs pushed on, hiding in caves and gullies from British aircraft. Suddenly, 'For no reason I was able to ascertain, they changed direction at right angles, and instead of completing the short distance to Gaza, they spent the night in open country, a long way from anything that mattered.'

Early the next morning HMS *Courageous* arrived at Jaffa from Malta carrying a battalion of soldiers. Trains rushed the troops to Gaza. Dobbie asked his political officers to find out why the Bedouin had changed direction. No rational explanation was ever discovered. For his part, Dobbie believed it was an answer to prayer. Without having resorted to martial law, he handed over a pacified Palestine to the new Commander-in-Chief, Air Vice-Marshal Dowding.

The British government was impressed, and commended Dobbie's handling of the 1929 Palestine Emergency.

The Bible calls the place where Christ was crucified 'the place of the skull.' Dobbie's office in Jerusalem looked out onto a hill often called 'Gordon's Calvary.' Back in 1883, General Gordon had noticed that this hill had the shape and appearance of a skull.

A Bible Society wished to distribute New Testaments to the brigade of British troops under Dobbie's command. He agreed, and in the office gazing at the hill looking like a skull, he wrote a statement to go with each New Testament. It reads:

You are stationed at the place where the central event in human history occurred – namely the crucifixion of the Son of God. You may see the place where this happened and you may read the details in this book. As you do this, you cannot help being interested, but your interest will change into something far deeper when you realise that the event concerns you personally. It was for your sake that the Son of God died on the cross here. The realisation of this fact cannot but produce a radical change in one's life – and the study of this book, will under God's guidance, help you to such a realisation.

Signed WGS Dobbie   Jerusalem
Brigadier   10th October 1929

His remaining tours of duty involved a few years as officer commanding the School of Military Engineering at Chatham. This was one of the highest specialist sapper appointments. After that he spent 1935 to 1939 in command of the fortress of Singapore. Here he realised that the potential enemy, the Japanese, could easily come in by the 'back door.' Funds for the defence of Singapore from an enemy invasion from the north were requested and refused. His attitude to the defence of Singapore was clear in his response when General Armitage told him, 'You might be the one to hand over Singapore to the Japanese.' Dobbie's reply was: 'We'll eat rats first.' Tragically, in 1941 the fortress fell in exactly the way he had foreseen.

God Himself will Fight for You

When World War Two started he was totally frustrated at being unable to do anything to help his beleaguered country. Then came the appointment to Malta.

The fighting power of Malta was quickly assessed. He commanded about 5,000 troops. At first there were only sixteen old anti-aircraft guns on the island. Four old Gladiator biplane fighters were discovered in disused crates. Three were assembled. They were nicknamed 'Faith,' 'Hope' and 'Charity.' For a time they provided the total air defence of Malta. Amazingly, one still survives in a museum on Malta.

Britain herself was under threat of invasion by Hitler in 1940. No reinforcements from home could be expected. The nearest British bases were Gibraltar, almost 1,000 miles west, and Alexandria, nearly 1,000 miles east. Instead, the most senior British army officer, Sir Edmund Ironside, sent a telegram from London. It said, 'Deuteronomy chapter three verse twenty-two.' Dobbie had a look at this verse in the Bible. It says, 'Do not fear them, for the Lord your God is the one fighting for you.'

Although Malta's future looked very uncertain, Dobbie the optimist always believed that Britain would win the war. He did not

The British Prime Minister Winston Churchill inspects air raid damage during a visit to the dockyard at Valletta on the island of Malta, 1942.

know how. Nor did Churchill.

When France was defeated by Germany in 1940, Dobbie addressed the Maltese people:

> *The decision of the British government to fight on until our enemies are defeated will have been heard with the greatest satisfaction by all the garrison of Malta. It may be that hard times lie ahead of us, but however hard they may be, I know that our courage and determination will not falter. With God's help we will maintain the security of this fortress I therefore call upon all of us to seek God's help, and then, in reliance on Him, to do our duty unflinchingly.*

Italy's declaration of war on Britain came on 10 June 1940. The first air raid on Malta followed at 6.00 a.m. the next day. Dobbie's broadcast to the Maltese people included these words: 'May God help us each one to do our duty unstintingly.'

Two hundred and seventy thousand Maltese heard what he said. The joke among them was that the people were more Catholic than the Pope. Yet both the population and their religious leaders liked and respected their decidedly Protestant governor. As a consequence, he gained and kept the full confidence of the Maltese people. This is a credit to him.

His straightforward honesty impressed them. He could be seen among crowds of hungry children, in the deep rock tunnels of the island, in the sun-baked streets of the towns, indeed anywhere there was need or trouble. He never resorted to a shelter. The raids did not cause him to cancel an activity. His courage was infectious.

Military historians today are astonished that Mussolini and Hitler failed to invade Malta, instead of trying to bomb it into submission. Both of the dictators had pre-arranged plans, but they were never implemented. Dobbie put it down to God's restraining hand. Whatever explanation is given, it is certain that failure to capture Malta resulted in the island being used by British submarines, ships and planes that sank numerous ships carrying supplies to enemy armies in North Africa. Rommel, the German commander, attributed much of the cause of his ultimate defeat in the battles for North Africa to the military performance of the fortress of Malta.

In his book *A Very Present Help* Dobbie records some incidents that made a big impression on him. One related to a convoy of supplies that reached Malta in January 1941. Among the convoy's escort ships was a new aircraft carrier, HMS *Illustrious*. This ship

Bomb damage in Valetta, Malta, 1 May 1942

limped into Malta already badly damaged by bombs. Once [over]
the dockyard, the German Luftwaffe decided to make sure she would
never leave Malta. They scored many hits. The prospects for saving
Illustrious looked small. After a while, the dockyard authorities
told Dobbie that if *there were* no *further damage* she could go to
sea in four days' time. Only Dobbie knew what the dockyard had
indicated. He prayed to God about it. He recorded:

The next day came. The attacks were renewed, but the Germans changed their tactics and bombed from a much greater height than before. They missed the ship – and no further damage was done. The same thing was experienced on the three following days and, eventually, on the fourth day, after sunset, I saw the great ship head for Alexandria, which she safely reached.

On another occasion the cruiser HMS *Penelope* had to enter dry dock in Malta for repairs. The enemy planes found her, like a sitting duck, helpless to avoid their bombs. *Penelope* was hit so often that her crew called her 'HMS *Pepper Pot*,' full of holes on top! The strange thing was that no vital damage was done. Necessary repairs were completed. Looking very much like a porcupine because of the large number of wooden plugs sticking out of her, she left Malta and fought her way to Gibraltar. On her arrival there was a service of thanksgiving on deck. Dobbie wrote, 'The whole thing was a miracle.'

In April 1942, while Dobbie was still governor, King George V1 awarded Malta the George Cross. This was the first of only two occasions in British history that an entire community has been honoured for valour. (The other was the Royal Ulster Constabulary in the twenty-first century.)

As the 2,300th air raid hit Malta on 7 May 1942, Dobbie was taken to Britain on the flying boat that brought in the next governor, Lord Gort. Four days later Dobbie was in hospital with a ruptured appendix. He was sixty-two.

Speaking at Malta's Council of Government, Gort summed up the story:

Malta owes much to Sir William Dobbie. It was he who organised this fortress for war. It was his foresight that produced the shelters. It was under his administration that the foundations were laid of the great civil organization which was destined to carry the siege through to a successful conclusion.

Dobbie died aged eighty-five on 3rd October 1964. He summed up the testimony of his life in these words: 'Vital and uninterrupted contact with our Heavenly Father is the most wonderful thing in the world.'

His faith in Christ was preserved through war and danger,

through fame and success, through bereavement and old age. That contact with God, rooted in Scripture, was never broken.

View of a 40mm Bofors anti-aircraft gun position overlooking Grand Harbour, Malta, 10 June 1942.

Arrival of General and Lady Dobbie at Rose Bay Air Base, Australia 1946.

11

The Reverend Lovell Pocock, Chaplain,

Royal Navy (1936–1963)

By Barry Shucksmith

The Reverend Frank Lovell Pocock, OBE, MA, Royal Navy, was the son of a Devonport vicar. He was educated at Christ's Hospital, Emmanuel College, and Ridley Hall, Cambridge, and after his theological training was ordained in Exeter Cathedral in December 1933. After his curacy, he considered the possibility of work overseas for the Lord, with particular interest in Kenya and Australia. These postings did not materialise, for Almighty God had other plans for His servant. After having supper with the Chaplain on an aircraft carrier, HMS *Furious*, Lovell was given a guided tour of the ship and was then taken to the Wardroom to meet a party of officers. They effectively 'press-ganged' him into the job of a Naval Chaplain. Lovell found their enthusiasm contagious and it moved him to volunteer. He joined at Devonport and within two months was appointed Chaplain of HMS *Woolwich*, destroyer depot ship in the Mediterranean. He served as a Naval Chaplain from 1936 to 1963.

Between 1939 and 1944, Lovell travelled to many parts of the United Kingdom, including the isles of Orkney and Shetland. He visited West Africa and South Africa (twice each), Aden, Sri Lanka, Malaysia, Singapore, Indonesia, Egypt, Malta, Gibraltar, and Sicily during the Sicily landings of July 1943. 'I had sailed in the North Atlantic, the Western Approaches, the South Atlantic, the Indian and Southern Oceans, the Arabian, the China, the Java, and the Mediterranean Seas. I had come through five years of war without a day's sickness or a single scratch. Three of the ships I sailed in had been sunk and I had lost my gear three times.'[36]

HMS *Ceres* and the Cold Arctic Waters

On 27th July 1939, Chaplain Pocock joined his first ship, HMS *Ceres*, for the Northern Patrol in the Arctic. War was on the horizon, the reserves were being called up, and so the younger chaplains had to go to sea immediately. The second-in-command at Deal told Lovell to 'Cheer up. We all hope that it will only be six weeks boating for the Reserve Fleet and then we shall all be back.' Such optimism seemed to pervade the pre-war atmosphere and, clearly, Lovell was not the only one reluctant to leave his happy station at Royal Marines, Deal.

The spring and summer of 1939 were anxious times. Germany seemed to be swallowing up most of Europe while Britain and France appeared to do nothing. However, King George VI and Queen Elizabeth still managed to visit Canada and the USA briefly. While there, the King and Queen attended a Christian gathering at the Department for Indian Affairs where Chief Whitefeather sang:

I'd rather have Jesus than silver or gold;
I'd rather have Jesus than riches untold;
I'd rather have Jesus than this world's fame;
I'd rather have Jesus and bear His shame.

Afterwards, the Queen thanked Chief Whitefeather and said that the words expressed her own thoughts and the King's, too. The royal couple's simple Christian testimony became world news, had a remarkable influence, and 'did us all a power of good,' wrote Lovell Pocock, on the eve of war.

To Sea from Woolwich

At that time, Pocock spoke of Royal Naval Volunteer Reserve members of his ships who were past retirement. Three older pensioners were commonly called 'The Three Musketeers' because, when not on duty, they propped themselves up on the bulkhead while smoking their pipes. When Lovell tried to obtain hymn cards for his services he could only get carols and these cards dated back to Queen Victoria's reign! For the commissioning of one of his ships, all he could do was to read a passage of Scripture, pray, sing from memory 'Eternal Father Strong to Save,' and end with the words of the Grace. Following a brief review by the King, on August 9th, the ships were out in the Channel day after day exercising with the rest of the Reserve Fleet.

War is Declared

'The Squadron anchored in Portland Harbour on Saturday, 2nd September. On Sunday 3rd September, all Ships' Companies assembled on their Quarter Decks to listen to the Prime Minister's address to the Nation at 11 a.m.. Mr Neville Chamberlain informed us that, as the German Army had not withdrawn from Poland and in spite of all his efforts we were now at war with Nazi Germany and that we would be fighting evil things.' Lovell movingly records, after his prayer for the ships' crews, 'I have never heard the word 'Amen' uttered from the hearts and throats of 500 men with such meaning. It was a thrilling experience and quite overwhelming.'

The young Naval Chaplain realised this was not the time to foster privilege and certainly not the time to hide behind his dog-collar. What would his role be? How would he rise to the occasion? What might he do to fulfil God's will for him? Everything was changing and changing fast. He had to go to his action station in the sickbay, respond to the ship's buzzers when the alarm went off in the middle of the night, and help to keep up the morale of the crew. The coming of war also meant visiting his 'parishioners' in the most dangerous of situations, not excluding the gun crews, damage control parties, and the hot, uncomfortable places below, where the stokers kept the boilers going day and night. His commission was to bring Jesus Christ to the men who served with him.

Courageous Survivors

On 17th September, Chaplain Pocock found himself helping to pick up survivors. HMS *Courageous* had been torpedoed 100 miles west of Ireland. It is a sobering thought that at the beginning of the War many of the ships did not have sufficient lifebelts. Tragically, 518 officers and ratings were lost when the 22,000-ton carrier was sunk and, unbelievably, the majority of *Courageous*'s ship's company were pensioners and non-swimmers. Lovell wrote of the comfort he found on returning home to Devonport by attending Evening Prayer. 'This simple act of worship, of reading the psalms for the day, of hearing the lessons read from the Old and New Testament and then joining in the ancient Collects (prayers), was quite overwhelming. It was satisfying and strengthening.' How true that, when the chips are down, the simplest act of worship, sincerely offered, with the

Lord Jesus Christ invited and present, can be holy ground indeed and a source of inspiration and help known only to the believing recipient.

Much more happened in the few short weeks before Christmas 1939 that was to test the young Chaplain not only as a minister of the Gospel but also as a Christian. Scapa Flow was not a safe anchorage for his squadron. A German submarine had managed to enter the 'Flow' and sunk battleship HMS *Royal Oak*, with the loss of about 800 lives. An attack by a German aeroplane that just missed them, the laying nearby of enemy magnetic mines, one of which made a substantial hole in HMS *Nelson*, and the dangerous situation created by Admiral Raeder, constituted a very real threat. The Admiral, Commander-in-Chief of the German Navy, ordered the *Scharnhorst* and the *Gneisenau* to patrol the same waters as Lovell's squadron, between Iceland and the Faroes. Yet, by the mercy of God, Lovell's ship *Ceres* sustained weather damage only and returned safely to Glasgow.

Christmas 1939 began with a carol service at Scapa Flow in the midst of a blizzard but, even then, the Chaplain wore his cassock, surplice, and scarf. The crew were dressed in oil-skins! Prayer, a carol, the blessing, and the National Anthem were about all they could manage in the appalling weather but the Lord upheld Lovell, the men responded well, and the true meaning of Christmas was proclaimed: 'It is a trustworthy statement, deserving full acceptance, that Christ Jesus came into the world to save sinners, among whom I am foremost of all.'[37] Later, 50 or 60 of the ship's company attended his Communion Service. The Chaplain was the youngest man in the ship. There he was, in this strange environment, seeking to bring his unique flock nearer to the Lord. At the end of the day he was able to give thanks for Christmas Day, for all that had happened: for preservation as a ship's company over the recent dangerous months, for the opportunity of bringing the saving love of Jesus Christ to such fine men, and 'finally for the love, constant care and affection with which we were surrounded, as shown by the enormous mail which arrived.' Lovell fell into his bunk and went to sleep peacefully with the words of a childhood carol in his mind:

Carol, carol, gaily,
Carol all the way;
Christ our loving Saviour,
Born on Christmas Day.

The Shock of a New Appointment – From Ice to Jungle

Within days, Lovell heard that the Chaplain of the Fleet was moving him from the 11th Cruiser Squadron to be the senior Chaplain of HM Naval Base, Singapore. This seemed ridiculous, a move from ice to jungle, after only a few short months. Such is life, not only in a blue suit, but as a messenger of God in the Armed Forces. Lovell reaffirmed his ordination vows and recalled the words of the Book of Common Prayer ordination service, 'Ye are called to be Messengers, Watchmen, Stewards, to teach, [forewarn], feed and provide for the Lord's sheep and to seek out the lost.' But the young Chaplain added, 'I fear I failed.' He was certainly being tested. He had been only nine months at the School of Music in Deal and now, after just seven months, he was being moved again. Lovell does not hide his anger and records a strong disagreement with the Chaplain of the Fleet. However, the Lord was dealing with him and making him more effective in one of the most difficult environments for Christian service.

Wake Up, Stand Fast, Repent and Get Ready

After leave, Lovell travelled to Singapore on HMS *Andes* and then got on a truck for a final, 25-mile journey through green jungle and around 59 horrific bends. However, he arrived to discover that the authorities had not been informed of his appointment and no provision had been made for his accommodation or work! Nonetheless, welcome or not welcome, Lovell was not going to be deterred from doing the Lord's work. He immediately visited three people: the Rear Admiral in charge of the Base, the Captain of Singapore Dockyard, and the Civil Secretary. The Civil Secretary seemed the most constructive in his comments. 'He suggested that I go to the stores and draw a Service bicycle!' When Lovell returned to the bungalow where he was to stay he found his luggage dumped there, but half of it was missing. Providentially, his Bible and Prayer Book were still there. He took them out of the container, read the Scriptures, prayed, and committed himself to the Lord, 'at the same time telling the Chinese servant to make him some tea' – the traditional British way of handling a crisis! The Lord had given him great peace but he now realised 'I was literally on my own. I knew nobody and… a Chaplain was the last person in the world the authorities expected to have on their hands.'

Chaplain Pocock was not going to be deterred by these discouragements. He set to work immediately to inform the Base he was present. He visited significant people, went to the hospital, looked up local clergy living in Singapore, and at the same time started Sunday and daily Services of worship. He was given the additional responsibility of censoring the mail.

Although in his early thirties, Lovell was exhausted most of the time but he persisted by the grace of Almighty God.

We kept the Day of Prayer called by the King in May. It would seem that 'The Miracle of Dunkirk' was God's answer to us. Humanly speaking the Army should never have got away. I took as a text 2 Chronicles, Chapter 7 verse 14; and as a thought 'Prayer moves the power that moves the world.' I exhorted our large congregation to join in faith with the whole Empire, in imploring God's mercy and help for the salvation of the British Army… The result was 'The Miracle of Dunkirk.'

One outcome of this particular service was that a number of dockyard folk, men and women, now started to attend church regularly.

By December 1941, Lovell had gathered large crowds to the church meetings. The situation in Singapore was deteriorating and the Japanese armies were getting nearer.

In November I began to impress on them the importance of keeping the four Sundays of Advent as a time of preparation for the Coming of the Lord; not only looking back to His birth at Bethlehem, but also looking forward to His coming again in judgement. I have been spelling out to them the fourfold message of Advent 'Wake up;' 'Stand fast;' 'Repent' and 'Be ready.' I have tried to teach them that the individual Christian believer and the congregation always face the world; materialism, the flesh; ourselves and the Devil; evil, hatred and the war. I warn them that any or all of these would take priority in the believer's heart instead of the Person of our Lord.

By now air raid sirens, Japanese aircraft engines, and a few loud sounds of bombs falling became more frequent. On 11th December

1941, two large ships, HMS *Prince of Wales* and HMS *Repulse,* left the base escorted by four destroyers. 'We heard the terrible news, from a radio, of the sinking of our two great ships, the *Prince of Wales* and *Repulse* by Japanese torpedo bombers and that our destroyers were picking up survivors.' Only 2,000 survivors returned to Singapore Base; hundreds and hundreds had been lost.

A new atmosphere began to pervade the naval base and people became more spiritually aware. Attendance at services increased. Lovell preached Christ to a packed church on Christmas Eve 1941:

> *Tonight I put it to myself and I put it to you that our first priority is not the Japanese closing in, or the blazing oil tanks, or even our own lives. The first priority is that Jesus Christ should be born and installed and established and enthroned in every heart here. I have no other message for you. 'He loved you and gave Himself for you.' Receive His word and receive Him… Receive His forgiveness and receive His presence. God be with you all, Amen.*

The Japanese were almost at the door. The exodus from Singapore took on a new pace. The Base had to be evacuated by 9.30 a.m. January 30th 1942. At 10.30 a.m. that day, 81 Japanese bombers attacked 7 targets in Singapore: the naval base, the 4 aerodromes, the city, and the docks. 'The arrival of the bombs was nerve-wracking but, once they were down, we knew we would have peace and quiet until the dark hours.' The Japanese also bombed Lovell's bungalow, leaving only the roof intact. He felt it was time to go, hurriedly packed what he could (his communion set, a few Christian books, and his clerical clothes), and joined HMS *Dragon,* one of the last ships out of port, not wishing to desert any of his flock. The whole situation was chaotic and a mad scramble. Singapore fell on 15th February 1942. Lovell arrived home safely in England during the first week of May 1942, ready for whatever the Lord had next.

Reconciled by the Cross

From May 1942 to June 1944 Lovell Pocock was Chaplain of the Second Mobile Naval Base Defence Organisation. He was to be based initially in the UK but with overseas responsibilities. This huge organisation of 10,000 men had its headquarters at Alton in Hampshire, but it also included the Air Defence Brigade, the Coastal

Artillery Regiment, and the Landing and Maintenance units, such as the Signals. There were four Church of England chaplains, as well as one Roman Catholic, one Church of Scotland, and one Free Church. Lovell was in charge as the Senior Chaplain. It was really an impossibly large task to meet the spiritual needs of so many. But, once again, Lovell set to visiting, sitting alongside the servicemen and talking, doing his 'spiritual rounds' in the outlying units, and visiting offices, the workshops, the galleys, the sickbay, and so on. In the evenings he would visit the different Messes and the recreation rooms and join in the games, seeking an opportunity to speak to the men about Christ.

On My Own and Wandering in the Desert

At the end of 1942, Lovell embarked on a large convoy of 60,000 men sailing for the Middle and Far East. After a brief stay in Durban, they sailed on through the Red Sea to Suez, where he boarded a train to Ismalia and then a truck to the Quassassin Desert.

Lovell was met by Italian prisoners of war and hundreds of Arabs. When working with the Royal Marines, Lovell had had to adapt and to find the best way to bring the Gospel to all the men. Now he again had to adapt to a completely strange environment. He was 'very much on [his] own,' however, 'fixing our eyes on Jesus, the author and perfecter of faith.'[38] Lovell took morning prayers, using passages of the Bible about Israelites wandering in the Desert and their deliverance under Moses to illustrate the Gospel.

On one occasion, during morning prayers, an Italian prisoner of war approached him carrying a wooden cross, which he had carved, and he put it in Lovell's hands.

> At that moment I felt quite overcome. Here was an enemy presenting me, a Minister of the Gospel, with the sign of God's forgiveness. I turned to the Marines and said 'This Italian prisoner has been preaching a sermon to us all; certainly to me. A year ago, in 1942, I was a survivor in a ship in the Indian Ocean. I lost everything except what I was wearing, and many others were in the same state, including a number of Royal Marines who were survivors from the Repulse and the Prince of Wales... God is speaking to us again, to all of us through this Italian prisoner...

I want to leave you all with a sentence of St Paul which comes to mind. 'Thanks be to God for His Indescribable Gift,' [39] *the Christ and His Cross.*

Soon after this, the young Lovell Pocock was almost killed. A military motorcycle, going at considerable speed in the depths of the dark night, collided with his tent: the tent pole collapsed and the tent was a write-off, but God protected His servant from any serious injury.

The Emotional Drain

Being a wartime Chaplain took a heavy toll on Pocock's energy and emotional reserves, not least in his having to try to help spiritually those who did not want to be there, against the backdrop of a terrible war. 'What a terrible, terrible world and as Oliver Goldsmith wrote, 'Where every prospect pleases and only man is vile,'" prayerfully records Lovell. 'The words of Psalm 79, verse 11 were often on my lips in those days,' says Chaplain Pocock, 'Let the groaning of the prisoner come before You… preserve those who are doomed to die.' His discussion groups during this time considered the passage from Scripture that said that 'the god of this world has blinded the minds of the unbelieving so that they might not see the light of the gospel of the glory of Christ, who is the image of God.'[40] It seemed to put everything into perspective.

Sitting on a Bomb – in Perils Often

Lovell and those with him knew that there was to be an assault on the Bay of Salerno, south of Naples, and it began on 9th September 1943. 'We embarked in a Landing Craft Transport (LCT) in Grand Harbour… The LCT had a Royal Navy crew. Those of us on the upper deck sincerely hoped we would not be hit by a shell, a bomb or torpedo during the crossing because the lower deck was like a huge petrol tank.' There can be few Christian ministers who have had to live with such daily danger. Yet the Apostle Paul spoke about many dangers he had to face in taking the Gospel into the most unlikely of situations. He penned 'three times I was shipwrecked… on frequent journeys, in dangers from rivers... dangers from my countrymen, dangers from the Gentiles...'[41]

On Christmas Day, 1943 in Augusta, the chaplains worked hard:

> *Speaking for myself, [wrote Lovell] the Christmas message, God was in Christ, went across well but the other half of the sentence, 'Reconciling the world unto Himself,' was still a long way off. The evil things we fought were still powerful. I had the feeling that there was great faith in our cause, and faith in God Himself, to see us through... About the turn of the year, 1943–1944, we heard that we would be returning home, disbanding and then reforming for the Second Front.*

The Struggle for Souls

At the end of January 1944, Lovell and his many Royal Marine friends embarked in a Dutch ship, SS *Sibajak*, manned by British officers and crew. This was Chaplain Pocock's ninth transport or trooper since 1939 and he had survived every threat, despite some very near misses. They arrived at Greenock with two other ships. Leave was granted to virtually everyone, yet the never-to-be-deterred Naval Chaplain stayed on to provide church services for those who were still on duty. Eventually, Lovell made his way to Chatham in a little Morris Eight, by courtesy of petrol coupons earned and as part of his Foreign Service leave! On arrival at Chatham, again he took the opportunity to examine himself spiritually, to read through the ordination service of the Book of Common Prayer (which he did annually), and to prepare prayerfully for the next move.

* * *

The war ended in May 1945. After a brief spell at the Royal Marines Barracks at Deal, Kent, he was assigned in March 1948 to HMS *Liverpool*. Joining this ship was not an easy move. It took time to adjust after the war years and leaving behind the Royal Marines. 'Within a few days I can remember thinking to myself "O my word! Fancy being locked up for two and a half years in this steel box with some of these people!"' Those of us who have done sea-time know the feeling. Others of us, who have served as Chaplains, or just as Christians, in the Forces, know also the additional problems brought by trying to serve the Lord in such confined and often very pagan circumstances. God's sovereign grace is as sure there, in one of His or Her Majesty's grey ships, as it is in the deepest and most unenlightened jungles of the tropics or the secular godlessness of the modern city.

The sea-going Chaplain has particular battles to fight.

I had gathered together about 20 men, two or three officers and the rest Ratings, into a loose Fellowship. Some of us used to read the Bible and pray, in the chapel, several days a week. However, they were all rather fearful and needed constant help and encouragement. So here I was in this great ship carrying 900 men; men who for the most part arrived in the service with no Christian faith; serving under a famous Admiral and travelling all round the Mediterranean. I realised that my task was to build up the church and preach the Gospel to the Ship's Company. I was determined to stick to my daily praying and meditation; to stick to my regular and systematic visiting of the various parts of the ship; and to try and shepherd my rather fearful flock who could easily err and stray when ashore in various ports we visited. A sentence from a book on the Battle of Midway, the battle which changed the course of the war in the Pacific in 1942, written by an American was, and has been, a great help to me over the years. He wrote 'A battle is only a battle when there is a crisis. Until then it is only an engagement.' I was in crisis and therefore engaged in battle. To quote John Bunyan, it was 'The struggle of mansoul;' for the souls of HMS Liverpool.

Chaplain Pocock also found the prayer that Sir Francis Drake had composed for the Battle of Cadiz in 1585 extremely helpful: 'Grant us to know that it is not the beginning, but the continuing of the same until it be thoroughly finished that yieldeth the true glory.'

Surprise, Surprise

One day Lovell was asked, 'Have you got the sermon ready for the great day tomorrow?' For Lovell it was just a normal Sunday. No one had told him until this late moment that Princess Elizabeth (our present Queen) had just arrived in Malta and would be attending Lovell's morning service on board HMS *Liverpool*. Virtually the whole ship's company would be present. While Lovell was waiting for the boat to arrive with the future Queen, Commander Topp (a true believer), who was waiting at the gangway to welcome the Princess on board, movingly said to the waiting Chaplain, 'My dear Parson, I hope that you can make the most of this great opportunity to preach the Gospel not only to the Princess but also to these hundreds of sailors.' Pocock didn't answer for a few seconds and then replied, 'I shall do my best.' This was a double surprise – and a threefold opportunity if ever there was one – to preach the saving grace of Jesus Christ to sinners, to the future monarch, and to the whole ship's company. The whole Grand Harbour of Malta rang with hymns and Lovell preached his sermon, based on the text he had already chosen days before. He did not deviate one bit. 'But the one who endures to the end, he will be saved.'[42] In fact, the Princess came to church in HMS *Liverpool* several times after this, including the end-of-year carol service.

Onward and Upward

Not the half has been told, but when eventually *Liverpool* had to go into dry dock for repairs, Lovell was not deterred from his work. He continued to conduct worship on board and recalls a Good Friday service at which the Sub-Lieutenant of the gunroom sang, 'Were you there when they crucified my Lord?' There was hardly a dry eye and yet they were in a dry dock!

From 1952 to 1955, Chaplain Pocock was at HMS *Siskin*, the Royal Navy Air Station at Gosport. He got involved with a missionary campaign at Harringay and many of his flock were converted. They went on to serve the Lord in the Royal Navy and, after discharge in local churches, scattered all over the nation. Four hundred turned up to a special service on one occasion, such was the moving of the Spirit. It seemed to be onward and upward now for the Royal Naval Chaplain, as if the Lord was rewarding and encouraging him for the lean years of the war. Dr Geoffrey Fisher, a personal friend of Lovell, wrote of the Harringay Mission in his Canterbury Diocesan notes:

The Vice Admiral commanding the 15th Cruiser Squadron, his wife and HRH The Duchess of Edinburgh. Andrew Blake HMS Liverpool 1950.

That the blessing of the Holy Spirit has been upon this campaign cannot be doubted. The mission itself has beyond doubt brought new strength and hope in Christ to multitudes and won many to Him, and for this God be praised.

Lovell's ministry with the Royal Navy ended in 1963, after a three-year appointment at HMS *Heron*, the Royal Navy Air Station at Yeovilton in Somerset. The Lord so richly blessed his ministry that the church building had to be re-constructed and extended.

To Live is Christ and to Die is Gain

Perhaps the secret of the Lord's blessing on Lovell Pocock is revealed when he quotes some words, almost at the end of his book, given to him by a clergyman friend. The words come from one of Bishop Stephen Neill's books, in which he recommends a daily routine for ministers: 'Two hours on your knees praying and four hours on your feet visiting.'

I know from personal experience, Lovell Pocock – now in glory with the Lord and Saviour he loved so deeply – put these words into practice.

Lovell confessed openly that the easiest thing is for a Chaplain not to pray. However, he was careful not to neglect his own walk with the Lord. He rose early every morning to lead daily prayers and read the Bible until 10.30 a.m.. At all his meetings he ensured that the Scriptures were read and that the Gospel was preached. He strove to obey the Lord Jesus Christ's command, 'seek first His kingdom and His righteousness,'[43] against tremendous odds.

I will also never forget the moment, when I cannot have been more than seventeen years old, when he suddenly laid his hands upon me in the side chapel of the Depot Church at the Royal Marines School of Music, Deal and prayed with great fervency for the Lord's blessing to be upon my life.

He was one of the most humble people I have ever known: not an ivory-tower figure at all, but one who rubbed shoulders with royalty, admirals, and the ordinary 'Jolly Jack Tar.' For him, as for the Apostle Paul, 'to live is Christ and to die is gain.'[44] There is no greater calling and no greater aim in life.

We are saved by grace alone, through faith alone, and in Christ alone. By this same grace, I shall see Lovell again in heaven. The even greater wonder is, 'when He appears, we will be like Him.'[45]

12

Siegfried Schäfer

Underneath You are the Everlasting Arms

By Siegfried Schäfer,
edited by Michael Claydon

Siegfried Schäfer is a Christian who served in the German Navy in the Second World War. After the conflict ended, he was a prisoner of war under the Russians for four years before he finally returned home and married his fiancée, Lydia. By his kind permission, his personal testimony of God's deliverance, focusing on his time in the navy, has now been published for the first time.

The Schäfer family now live in Gütersloh, Germany and he celebrated his 90th birthday in 2012.

* * *

As I look back over these events, the passage from Deuteronomy 33:27 comes to mind as a fitting heading: 'The eternal God is a dwelling place, and underneath are the everlasting arms.'

Lydia and I have both experienced the truth of this godly promise on our journey to the present day and I have followed Lydia's wish for me to describe the events of 14th May 1944. The original record was written during my stay in the Netherlands at the beginning of February 1945.

I will open my mouth in a parable; I will utter dark sayings of old, which we have heard and known, and our fathers have told us. We will not conceal them from their children, but tell to the generation to come the praises of the Lord, and His strength and His wondrous works that He has done.[46]

This is also the central idea with which I pass on this account so that it can be used for the glory of He who is still able to perform miracles today.

* * *

Praise the Lord, O my Soul!

It is Saturday, 13th May 1944. Tomorrow it will be four weeks to the day since I bade farewell to my loved ones back home and since Lydia, my fiancée, waved to me as we departed until we lost sight of each other.

That was four weeks ago – and today? We're stationed in Borkum with our three minesweepers[47] and have now been at sea for almost four weeks. The swell of the sea has occasionally presented itself as my adversary. I have also seen the full force of war and thank the Lord that so far everything has gone well. The enemy bombed the boat next to us heavily and, on one occasion, the bombs went off in the water only 50–100 metres from our own boat.

I felt pressed this morning to write something about this experience to my fiancée. I wrote to her about the dangers of seafaring but also about Him who holds His hand over those He loves in every circumstance and how, despite all of this, I still have a happy heart in Him.

We were ready to set sail again, no one knew to where. Perhaps it was better that way; otherwise, I would have worried about the voyage. This was not the most pleasant of journeys. Too often we had heard of attacks by low-flying aircraft and enemy fast-attack boats had often been seen near Terschelling.

As we left Borkum and headed westwards, the sea was glassy. If there hadn't been a war on, the voyage could even have been fun. Now, however, there was only a bitter sobriety.

Sunday 14th May 1944. At midnight, my watch as helmsman began. The sea was so quiet that it did not require any effort on my part to keep the ship on course: I could go for minutes without having to move the rudder. After about an hour, we began to feel a slight rocking of the ship. We had thought that the sea-swell would remain at this low level, but how wrong we were! The movements increased and eventually became so strong that my compass was swinging 10–20 degrees either way with the swaying of the ship. I was able to keep myself composed until 4 a.m., by which time my midriff was rumbling alarmingly! At last my relief arrived, Seaman 1st Class Decker.

After a short and fitful sleep, the port watch again reported for duty and I went with them up to the bridge, declaring, 'Seaman 1st Class Schäfer, reporting for duty as helmsman, course 20 degrees.'

The swell had increased yet further. 'Have fun,' Decker taunted me as I took over the helm.

I suppose I lasted an hour before I had to ask someone else to take the helm. I hurried over to the side and held my whole upper body over the edge – what could possibly be demanded from an empty stomach? There was nothing to give! The Officer of the Watch saw me and told me to go below. I didn't need telling twice! Taking a hammock, I spread it between the lockers and lay down but sleep would not come.

It seemed impossible, but the swell increased even further. A storm warning had been given hours ago and now the convoy had turned round and was heading back to Borkum. We had to travel at the speed of the slowest cargo ship, which (with the swell) meant that we were practically creeping along.

When the port-side sentries were called up at 12:20 p.m., a hammock became free. I lay down but could not sleep. It was probably about 1 p.m. when I finally fell asleep, but my rest would not last long.

Times of Trouble

At 13:22, the alarm bells sounded on deck. An air raid! I leapt out of the hammock, my seasickness gone in an instant. Quick, to the guns! As we reached the deck there was a loud bang and a flash of light. No one knew what was happening. Before we could compose ourselves, the shout of 'fire on board' rang out. Yes, but where? No one knew. Steam was pouring out of the second boiler room: something must have happened to the boiler.

Everyone was running around like a headless chicken. The herd instinct of humankind showed itself as one man went to the upper deck and everyone followed. Of course, there was still the air raid alarm: we were still under attack! I went up to my action station: the midship 2cm guns on the superstructure.

As I went reached the deck I found the gunners already there. 'What happened?' I asked. 'Look there, starboard side.' I saw that a cargo ship from our convoy had been hit amidships by a bomb. It was breaking apart: the bow and stern were above the water as the ship sank. 'What about us?' I asked. 'We've been attacked by low-flying aircraft.' We examined the gun and tried to get it ready again but it wouldn't cock. A piece had been torn off: a shot must have hit it directly on the loading mechanism.

Gradually we pieced together what had happened: three Bristol Blenheim fighter-bombers flying very low over the water had attacked us from the port side with 4cm guns. As the ship was listing to starboard, the aircraft raked the whole side of the ship with gunfire below the waterline. Judging by the head-sized holes in the ship's side, they must have been using some form of high-explosive shells.

The damage control team was diligently trying to seal up the damaged parts of the ship. The wedges bashed in were still holding, but what could be done about the larger holes? The raging swell of the sea was not letting up and the great mass of flowing water was scarcely curbed by the team's attempts to cover the gaping holes with canvas.

Beaufighter aircraft of No. 455 Squadron RAAF took part in this attack against a German minesweeper in the heavily defended Den Helder anchorage in the North Sea.

This was not the only threat to our survival. So much water had poured into the boiler room that the fire had been extinguished: we were unable to move, and all this near the shore in a stormy sea.

As the convoy struggled on towards Borkum, Ship *M369* from our flotilla, under Commander Vogt, stayed behind to give us help. She came alongside us so that a towing cable could be attached. At the appropriate distance, a heaving line was thrown but the first attempt failed. Commander Vogt tried again. He came so close that, with the raging swell of the sea, the masts threatened to break off both ships. This time the throw was successful and we managed to pass a good towing cable between the heavily pitching ships. Slowly, we started on our journey again. Everyone was breathing much easier as we set off again towards Borkum.

The large bilge pump had also broken. This meant that everyone had to carry buckets and whatever containers they could find to bail out the water. I was standing in the dirty water in the boiler room, passing bucket after bucket up to the deck. All I could hear was the rushing of water going this way and that, the rumbling coals, and the clashing shovels. Yet, despite everything, and despite the tightness of the boiler room, down there I felt nothing of my previous wretchedness. In His time the Lord is always near to His own. I had often felt this and, in that particular moment, I felt it again.

I was eventually relieved of my task and, arriving on the top deck, I saw that every unnecessary item was being thrown overboard: bullet magazines, wire, mine-sweeping devices – everything that couldn't float was being thrown over the side. Comrades were having hurried discussions: 'We can't keep this anymore,' said one and another, 'In one to two hours, we'll have to chuck it.' Despite the circumstances, I did not find the situation too bad. I'm certain that the Lord had given me great peace in this situation. To His honour I must say that in that moment I was never afraid. He gave me the ability to trust wholly and completely in Him.

We were still listing to port. The Commander directed that the motorised dinghy be cut free. A few men cut the ties that held the dinghy in its davits. With one swing the dinghy drifted off, but the ship still did not right herself. Every second that passed felt like an hour.

'Hard to port! Hard to port!' Sub-Lieutenant Fock commanded loudly so that everyone on board could hear. 'Tell everyone down there to move the rudder to the port side!' However, the steering mechanism worked no longer. As another wave pounded the port side, the ship reached her capsizing point. Her fate was sealed.

Into the Deep

Immediately understanding the situation, Sub-Lieutenant Fock calmly and clearly gave his orders: 'Rafts and inflatable dinghies overboard! Save the wounded! Abandon ship!'

Everyone's nerves were tense to the extreme. Most of the crew didn't bother with the rafts or the dinghies but instead jumped straight into the water from the port side, which, by now, was very close to the waterline. Others were running to the starboard side. That was the better decision, as whoever jumped off the starboard side had more of a chance to swim away from the suction caused by the sinking ship.

Three of us threw three life rafts overboard from the middle of the ship. Due to the listing of the ship, we had to throw them into the water on the port side. I then set about inflating my life jacket, as it was now high time to abandon ship. Without any kind of fear, I went past the port-side guns, which were almost under water. With one small step I was in the North Sea.

I swam towards the nearest raft and reached it quite quickly. Already some of my comrades were clinging to this raft and more were coming over. The raft was gradually sinking, as there were too many holding onto it.

Another raft drifted by to my right. I let go of mine and grabbed the new one, but above me was the funnel of the ship and, as she sank, so the funnel got closer and closer to where I was swimming. I couldn't swim away because of the currents and eddies. What should I do? Just in front of me was a third raft, so I left the second one and tried to swim towards it. As I rolled into the water, my life jacket tore and the two parts separated. I started to sink deeper until the water was right up to my chin.

My thoughts were immediately for my loved ones back home. 'Was yesterday's letter to you, Lydia, an unintentional farewell-letter?' I put into practice the command to 'call upon Me in the day of trouble; I shall rescue you, and you will honour Me.'[48] As I prayed, I recalled the verse from Psalm 91 that a Christian brother had sent me, which ended with the promise, 'A thousand may fall at your side and ten thousand at your right hand, but it shall not approach you.'[49]

The Lord had His plan for my loved ones and me. I didn't have to strain to get to the desired raft because He made it come towards me on a wave and I cried out, 'Oh thank you, Lord' from the bottom of my heart.

I grabbed hold of the raft and climbed straight in. The funnel of the ship was still hovering above me. I tried, in vain, to paddle away. 'Oh Lord, you've already saved me in such a wonderful way, please help me again, now!' Once again He heard my pleas and, riding one of the waves, I was able to move the raft away from the funnel and get out of the wake of the ship as it sank. During this whole rescue, my short words of thanks were just a stammer: I couldn't say any more than that. I had experienced His goodness close to me.

As I drifted, I thought through what had just actually happened: 'You didn't really do anything yourself at all. Wasn't it as though an invisible hand had been leading and guiding everything? It showed you the way from raft to raft. You're a non-swimmer too and yet you remained above the water. Oh Lord, it was You who directed everything so gloriously. I did nothing and everything came from You!'

From my raft I watched the sinking of our ship. Three hours earlier we had directed our guns at the enemy planes and shot one down. And now? Everything was silent. Only the gurgling and rushing of water was audible. The bow was looming out of the water; then, finally, after a few moments, our ship was no more to be seen.

My raft drifted on and towards Seaman 1st Class Binder. I managed to pull up alongside him. It drifted on further to Sub-Lieutenant Fock. He wore a heavy leather jacket and it was difficult to haul him aboard the raft, but we managed.

A little distance away we drifted past Seaman 1st Class Ulbricht. His shouts of 'I can't go on much longer! I can't do it!' rang out in our ears but, unfortunately, we weren't able to help him. The swell of the sea was too strong and we had to leave many of our comrades in the water. Across the whole of the disaster area you could hear the whistles of individual comrades who were swimming in the water. With the cries for help and the rushing of the sea, there was a peculiar but harrowing melody. It is only with difficulty that I'm able to get that sound out of my mind.

When we were given the command to abandon ship, Commander Vogt had cut the towing cable with the other ship. Then he turned around and began the rescue operation.

A number of our shipwrecked comrades were already on the rescue ship when the three of us drifted past in our little boat. One of the kitchen hands threw a line to us but it was too short. When he tried to throw it again, we had drifted off away from the ship. Sub-Lieutenant Fock tried to calm us, and perhaps himself as well: 'We'll make it. We're safe for now.' He was calmness personified and, with the paddle in his hand, he kept the boat pointing in the direction of the rescue ship.

We were becoming increasingly concerned that we were drifting further and further away from the rescue ship. Soon it was over 1,000 metres away from us. We alternated between being full of hope and full of fear. Would they even see us from the ship? Wait: now they seemed to be turning towards us. We started waving with the paddle but they turned away again.

The swell was simply indescribable. The sea appeared to fly into a rage. We drifted towards the coast and ended up in the middle of the surge. In front of us was a four- to six-metre-high wave. No sooner had we braced ourselves than the crest crashed over us. Then we were back in the valley between waves.

There were provisions on the raft. Sub-Lieutenant Fock thought that we'd be able to hold out for the night. He was a professional sailor and so could be trusted. I, however, as a child of God, entrusted myself wholly and completely to my Saviour, to whom I would sing, with a thankful heart, 'How great is your Almighty goodness.'

Then, finally, our time had come and we were next in line to be rescued. This time it was unmistakeable from the markings on the mast that they were headed for us. Just in front of our raft, the *M369* turned to port so that we were on her starboard side. Sub-Lieutenant Fock got out first. I went next, but the raft was bobbing about, up and down. You had to catch the most opportune moment to grab hold of the railings, which I did, but only on the third attempt. I could only hold on with one hand, but three or four arms lifted me aboard over the railings. I could do nothing but say, 'Thank you, Lord.'

Wonderfully, he had saved me from the floods of the North Sea, which was often justifiably called the 'Death Sea.' Now He would allow me to see you, Lydia, and my parents again.

I went down to the bunks and took off all my wet clothes. The comrades on the *M369* proved themselves very helpful. One of them directed me immediately towards a free bunk at the officers' end, down from the ladder-way. I wrapped myself tightly in the blanket I'd been given, just as a severe chill came over me. Despite all of this, my heart was rejoicing and praising the Lord, who had done so much good for me.

We arrived in Borkum and the wounded were the first to be taken off the ship. Then, with one swing, I was off. Finally, I had solid ground under my feet – what a feeling! 'Lord, I thank You once more from the bottom of my heart!'

Saturday 20th May 1944: I'm at home and quite busy ironing my clothes. I saw my Lydia as she arrived on her bicycle. My mother left the kitchen and soon we were in each other's arms, so all of this is a fact. I'm back with you, Lydia. The Lord has led everything wonderfully. He will also continue to lead us wonderfully, according to his wise council. How did the psalmist put it in Psalm 121:8? 'The Lord will guard your going out and your coming in from this time forth and forever.'

Siegfried Schäfer pictured in 2012.

13

Colonel Robbie Hall QGM

Through Perils in the Deep

By Colonel Robbie Hall QGM

The stage for my drama was set during the London Blitz in 1941. Urban gasworks provided a popular target for the German bombers. A direct hit caused considerable collateral damage and targeted Britain's war effort at home. During a blackout, bombers would approach London by following the River Thames, which brought into view Beckton Gas Works in East London. An early hit on the gasworks would light up London's East End, paving the way for further attacks.

The heavy steel nose cone of the German 500kg SC 500 bomb was designed to penetrate deep into the foundations of buildings before exploding, maximising its destructive effect. The domed, steel-plate crown of Gasometer 4 at Beckton[50] did not even slow the bomb's progress as it careered through the gas-filled void and down into the deep water sump underneath. Its slight angle of descent as it passed through the water sump turned the bomb on its side, causing it to smash sideways through the concrete lining at the base. Not designed to withstand such lateral forces, the nose section of the bomb broke away and rolled down the sloping surface at the base of the sump and out to its edge. The main body of the bomb lay closer to the centre, fixed in the London clay, with only a bomb-shaped hole in the concrete to mark its position.

After the bombing raid, the two-foot-diameter entry hole in the crown was quickly patched, along with all the other holes in the gasometers, and the tank was restored to normal function after only the briefest of interruptions. No one was aware of the large, unexploded bomb still inside Gasometer 4.

Like most German bombs of the Second World War, the fuse of the SC 500 is located in a steel pocket in the centre of the bomb's body. The fuse is electrical, with a switching mechanism designed to operate as the bomb impacted. It is likely that, on this occasion, the fuse failed to function simply because the bomb had flipped sideways as it passed through the water. Consequently, the bomb remained in a state of near-perfect preservation for 45 years. Meanwhile, the delicate explosives in the fuse pocket degraded and crystallised, becoming ever more volatile.

All of this was more than a decade before I was born and yet my own path as a military diver and Bomb Disposal Officer in our modern Army was to confront this legacy of a former generation's war. It was in the Army that I learned that there is an all-powerful God, that He cares for us individually, and that He has a plan and a purpose even for someone like me, one who had denied God and strayed far from any semblance of a godly life. I have since come to the conclusion that God required all of the 500kg of TNT in the Beckton bomb to get through my thick skull with His message of love in Christ Jesus!

The Alarm is Raised

I had specialised as a diver early in my Army career, during my first tour as a young Troop Commander. The divers' training course is notoriously tough and testing. Being a fit, strong mountaineer certainly helped, but the course was 'hard-man' territory where considerable resilience was required to cope with prolonged physical exertion, discomfort, and fear. In addition to all of this were endless studies of diving physics and physiology and, for officers, swathes of regulations and procedures that all had to be learnt. This training and the several years of operational diving that followed provided something of a journey of experience that led to the Beckton incident. However, it was at Beckton that the infinitely more important journey, my journey to God, was to begin.

By chance, the heavy steel nose of the bomb had come to rest with its point facing upwards and this had prevented the gasometer's inner lift[51] from being lowered completely. For 45 years, the gasworks' engineers could not understand why the lift would not descend the final eighteen inches. It was in fact because the full weight of the gasometer was resting on the bomb's nose. Eventually, in 1986, the nose poked a hole through the base of the inner lift, rupturing the gasometer and causing a gas leak.

Internal repairs to gasometers are quite rare and, for obvious reasons, are delicate and complicated. It was decided that a commercial diving team was needed to find and remove the obstruction that had caused the damage. The specialist commercial diver was a former Royal Marine who was experienced at working in gasometers. As he felt the distinctive shape of the nose cone, he immediately recognised it to be a bomb. The repair team made a hasty withdrawal from the gasometer and raised the alarm.

When the call came, as is so often the case with a major incident, it was late on a Friday afternoon. I was on duty as the Senior Bomb Disposal Officer for 33 Engineer Regiment (Bomb Disposal) and also the regiment's Diving Officer.

I recall feeling slightly smug when we arrived and met one of the London-based bomb teams. They had been there for some time but had still been unable to get anywhere near to the suspected bomb and could only wait for the arrival of my diving team. However, rivalries were soon put aside and we set about working out evacuation plans and safety cordons.

With the agreement of the local police, I took command of the scene. We needed to focus on the diving task and were grateful for the support of the other, non-diving, disposal teams. They were able to help in a number of ways, leaving my team and I to concentrate our minds on what I soon realised was a very daunting problem. As the Chief Gas Works Engineer explained the situation, standing alongside the towering structure of the gasometer, I was left in awe at the scale of the task.

The commercial diver gave me a useful brief on the technical difficulties involved in diving in gasometers and on the numerous hazards. There was a very large amount of vitally important information to assimilate in a short space of time. As I started to formulate a plan and tease it out with the head engineer and my own team, my smugness was replaced by a grave sense of responsibility.

I had to develop a safe, sensible, and rational plan to resolve numerous complex issues in which the potential consequences of a wrong decision were very serious indeed. There was a danger that if an incident like this were not firmly gripped it would run out of control. Plans for widespread evacuation, road closures, and even a re-routing of the flight-path into Heathrow were being considered and all on the basis of a cone-shaped metal fragment discovered beneath a gasometer.

The gasometer was set at 'three lifts up,' providing a 'breathable' atmosphere to work in. Each lift was 40 feet high with a walkway around its upper rim. The walkway was reached by climbing fixed

Beckton Gasometer 4

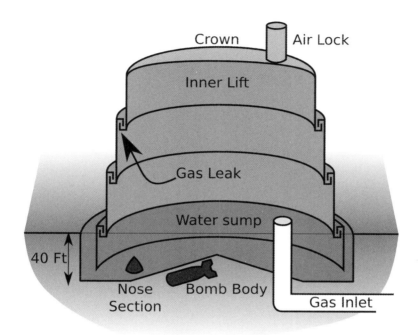

spiral ladders. Hauling the diving gear over the final ladder and onto the crown gave an appreciation of the true scale of these structures. The domed surface seemed vast, like an empty football field, with a conspicuous airlock standing several feet from the edge and a prominent winch and cable attached to the adjacent railing.

That night London's East End, the Docklands, and the far bank of the Thames were all clearly visible from where we stood, adding to the sense of height. Our colleagues from the police and the Gas Board, and a small crowd of other people, now appeared a long way off and were in touch only by radio. The sense of isolation increased enormously as we were winched down through the airlock one by one to a small, timber platform.

I had decided on a minimum team of four for this first

reconnaissance dive, which I would conduct, with two other divers and the senior Gas Board engineer in support. He was to prove crucial to our efforts at almost every step that night and over the coming days. Despite it being a small team, there was little room for manoeuvre and careful organisation was needed just to insert one diver into the water and onto the target.

The cavernous, windowless space was pitch black. Our torch beams picked out distant walls and various structural bracing bars around the vast space. I was able to identify the threatening gaps between the base of one lift and the top of the next. I appreciated the commercial diver's advice to stay clear of these and of the numerous underwater inlets and outlets. The 'breathable' air still smelled and tasted strongly of the gas that had filled the space for so many decades. We all developed severe headaches. Then there was the oil: black, old oil had been placed on the water for various functional reasons, but it spread absolutely everywhere and was unpleasant in the extreme.

The oil and many other toxic pollutants caused the soft rubber neck and cuff seals on our diving suits to perish and fall apart after only a few days. Breathing the air from the diving set was a pleasant relief.

Despite this environment, it was still with a sense of adventure that we located a small dinghy below the recently added repair patch on the base of the top lift and I finally entered the water.

A Despairing Cry

The sequence of pre-dive surface checks was curtailed as the smears of oil over my facemask made the torchlight dazzling. I hastily vented my suit but, as I descended below the surface, the most awful sense of horror and panic hit me.

The diving set was not designed to cope with such contaminated water. The mouthpiece relies on a simple diaphragm seal to keep water out and to allow air in from the cylinders. However, as I passed down through the surface and breathed in, a mix of oil and grit was drawn into my breathing apparatus.

I inhaled the foul mixture with my first full breath. The other members of the team were oblivious to my crisis several feet below the oily, black surface, but it was their presence that concentrated my mind and held back my instinct to fight for the surface, tear off my facemask, and abort the whole ridiculous venture. Had I done so, the impact on my credibility and personal confidence would have been such that I doubt that I would have dived again on that operation, or at all. I thank God that another instinct took over.

Choking, dizzy, disorientated, and with vomit forming at the base of my throat, I prayed. Although I had always believed that there was a God, I had never until then considered that God could have any contemporary relevance to me as an individual. He had created an amazing universe, given light and life to it, and even put mankind on the Earth. However, I had always thought my time in this life was what I made of it, with some influence of chance, for good or bad. God was remote. For these reasons my prayer was not a 'believer's prayer,' but it was an earnest one! It was also an answered one.

As I continued to descend, I simultaneously exhaled and vomited through my mouthpiece with every last breath I could muster and then automatically inhaled deeply. The relief I felt as my lungs filled with clean air was overwhelming; there were tears of joy in my eyes as I thanked the God who had just saved me from drowning in lungsful of filthy oil. Although the technical explanation was simply that my vigorous exhalation had cleared the diaphragm, allowing air to flow from my cylinders, a very significant and miraculous change had taken place in my mind and spirit.

All sense of fear, uncertainty, and a constant concern for my personal esteem had been suddenly replaced by a new composure and sense of purpose. I realised that this place and this job were exactly where God had placed me and what He had prepared me for.

There is a tremendous sense of privilege in knowing you are part of God's plan, however small that part may appear to be. I did not know the words of the Bible at the time of this experience, but appreciate now the weight of truth and assurance in the promise that God knows each of us in the smallest detail:

O Lord, *You have searched me and known me…. If I make my bed in [hell], behold, You are there.*[52]

There is no place or situation, even for a diver lost in the pitch-black bowels of an old gasometer, that can hide us from His presence.

From that moment I had no more uncertainty. I knew exactly what had to be done and I was equally certain that all would be well with me and my team on this operation. I continued the dive with a new assurance of God's presence; this assurance has remained with me to this very day.

I quickly found the conical, steel shape and confirmed it to be the nose cone of a large German bomb from the Second World War. We hauled it to the surface and took it out of the gasometer. We established that the nose was not a fragment of a bomb that had landed outside the gasometer and been blown through its side wall. We knew, therefore, that the main body of the bomb must still be inside, complete with most of the 500kg of TNT filling and, importantly, the fuse with its associated gain explosives, by now much degraded and very sensitive. It took two further days of searching the base of the gasometer before the bomb's body was found by the most junior diver on the team. He literally fell through the hole in the concrete and landed on top of it.

The situation was unique and some of the normal diving and bomb disposal rules and procedures had to be adapted. We broke with convention and moved the bomb to the surface of the water before attempting to defuse it. The three-man team that I chose for this high-risk phase was considered by some as being too small to conduct a confined-space diving operation safely and by others to be placing too many in the proximity of a fuse during the delicate immunisation process. It proved to be a sensible compromise and meant at least I had someone to hold the torch and keep the dinghy steady while I focused on the delicate operation on the fuse.

The operation was entirely successful, with but one other heart-stopping moment: as I drilled into the fuse pocket with a fine hand-drill, there was a sudden hiss as air rushed into the vacuum. Once the fuse immunisation and two-hour soak period were complete, we began the painstaking process of extracting the bomb body through the air-lock to a remote area of waste ground, where the bulk explosive was liquefied by a steam heater and removed.

This left only the steel fuse pocket in the centre of the heavy casing, which we destroyed with a controlled explosion. The blast tore and twisted the thick, steel casing beyond all recognition and was a sobering reminder of the need to treat these older fuses with very great care. We looked at one another in silent acknowledgement of the very real danger that had threatened us all.

My experience during that initial dive remained at the forefront of my mind throughout the long and testing operation. I had been changed from someone who acted impulsively and was something of a 'show off' to one who was genuinely prayerful and considered in his actions. I remained grateful to God and sensed that a personal journey to true faith in Him had begun.

I had learned that God is not remote, but cares for each of us as an individual. I knew God to be both relevant to and interested in our daily lives; I saw Him as a guide and protector. My own human frailty had been very clearly shown to me, but I was no longer concerned, as this bomb disposal officer and diver now had a most powerful 'ally.'

I now realise how small a step I had taken towards the true faith that comes with the knowledge of Jesus Christ, but then and for some time to come I was convinced, as were my family, friends, and colleagues, that I had 'found God.' Happily, the story does not end there.

Christ is the Key

Some months later, a national radio station called my regiment, asking for a Christian bomb-disposal expert to be interviewed for one of a series of broadcasts featuring Christians in hazardous occupations. By this time my new faith was quite well known. I had talked about it openly and had regularly attended the Garrison Church. Consequently, my name was instantly offered.

Jesus's name was not mentioned in the broadcast, for the simple reason that, at this stage, I did not know Him! I sought to acknowledge and to honour God's comfort and assurance that I had experienced during and continued to experience since the Beckton drama. However, it was revealing that, when asked to select a piece of music to round off the interview, I chose 'My Way' by Frank Sinatra.

It was obvious to genuine Christian friends that I still had much to learn. Shortly before I departed to the Falkland Islands for another tour of duty, one of these good Christian friends was able to share with me that 'Jesus is the key.'

Unlike my earlier tour in the Falklands, these six months passed at a relatively easy pace, with only an occasional foray out to the well-fenced minefields for which I was responsible. It was a God-given opportunity to learn the claims and convictions of true Christian faith and to make my own informed choice for Christ.

By God's good provision, there was a place known as *The Oasis*, run by the Mission to Military Garrisons, where a small group met to study the Bible. I sat at the back of the small group, listening intently and learning the message of the Christian Gospel. Within a couple of months I was a true believer in the saving grace of the Lord Jesus and was running the study group.

It is true to say that there were some hurdles to overcome along the way. It took the truth of Scripture (particularly in Romans Chapter 1) for this 'do-gooder' to see the depth of my own sin, in common with that of all my fellow men, and the enormous gap that separated me from our creator, God, the very benchmark of all that is good, right, and holy.

I came to be in no doubt that I had irrevocably strayed from His presence. My rescue by Him at Beckton was in fact a call to turn and to seek Him. I had to learn that this rescue was out of His love for me and utterly undeserved. My prayer had been a genuine and earnest one and I know that it was answered. However, more importantly, the Lord was calling me to recognise the infinitely greater danger I was in: that of ending this life with my sin still an eternal barrier to entering the presence of a Holy God. In those Bible studies I learned that God Himself has removed such a barrier for any and all repentant people, through Jesus Christ at the Cross. My friend was so right in saying, 'Jesus is the key.'

I struggled for a time, as have others, with the identity of Jesus Christ and understanding how on the Cross He could bear the fierce anger of God which otherwise was my due. This seemed to be unfair. Many a good soldier will insist on facing his own due punishment rather than letting another carry it for him. However, I joined the Falklands Island group at the perfect time, just as they were studying chapter one of John's Gospel. There could have been few better passages to begin to understand that Jesus Christ was in fact God and that He had died as my substitute.

I read in John's Gospel statements about Jesus Christ such as, 'He was in the beginning with God. All things came into being through Him,' and that 'He came to His own…;' and that 'But as many as received Him, to them He gave the right to become children of God, *even* to those who believe in His name.'[53] Elsewhere, I read where the

Bible calls Him 'Immanuel,'[54] which means 'God with us.' I realised that Jesus Christ was not just another 'ordinary' baby, but was God Himself who had become a man.

Then I came to understand that the baby grew up and, at the appointed time, He was executed on the Cross, bearing in full the punishment for our sin. God did not lay the burden on another, but Jesus Christ, God Himself, bore the full penalty for *my* sin and for that reason I could be forgiven.

I remember clearly the day and the hour, on 8th December 1988, when I came to accept this. I knelt at my bed to acknowledge my sin and committed all that I was and had to the Lord Jesus Christ as the only way to salvation.

My dear, long-suffering wife had long endured the anxieties of bomb disposal, often for hours and days, when for me the crisis point lasted only moments. She saw a changed man come home after the Beckton bomb and, in the main, was pleased with the results. It was good to have a husband who would now take her to church. However, the husband who then wrote from the Falkland Islands and returned soon after was truly changed.

My next perilous task was to explain to this good, church-going lady the dangers of a church life that was not fully centred on Christ. Our eight-year old son got there first, having listened to our conversations, but I had a certain assurance that my wife was part of God's perfect plan from the outset. She too found faith through understanding what is written for us so clearly in the Bible.

Epilogue

It was clearly God's purpose to keep me involved in military diving and bomb disposal as the Army's capability developed and grew enormously over the following years. I became the first-ever Army Commander of the Royal Navy Diving School. Some years later, when the Army could not produce enough operators to meet the burgeoning requirement of Afghanistan and the terrible casualties caused by Taliban bombs, I knew well that the Royal Navy Clearance Divers would be both able and willing to lend their support. The Royal Air Force Bomb Disposal Branch also added their efforts and I was given the task of enabling all of these diverse elements to work as one, through a single training programme. This was my challenge and privilege over the last four years of my Army career.

I immediately launched myself into a one-year Master's Degree programme in Bible and Mission and the experience was sufficiently intense to cushion me from any negative emotions at leaving the Services, whilst preparing me to expand my service for Christ. Local church leadership and ministry, with some wider responsibilities within the military Christian organisations, are gelling into God's plan for me for the future. He is certainly not finished with me yet. My three serving sons (a military doctor, an engineer, and a trainee helicopter pilot) prevent me ever missing the Army, even for a moment. They too have trusted in the God who heard my prayer in the depths of Gasometer 4 at Beckton.

Colonel Hall QGM (second from right) pictured with his family.

14

Guardsman 'Jack' Ringer

Bookmaker Turned Missionary

By Michael Claydon

On 27th June 1904, Walter John Ringer was born. To his father he was 'John' but to everyone else this infectiously enthusiastic lad was 'Jack.'

Following his father's death, the family returned to his maternal grandparents' home in Fakenham, Norfolk. Jack's new home proved to be a very happy and loving Christian environment and his grandmother was especially faithful in lifting Jack up to God in prayer. His mother insisted on Sunday school attendance despite the long walk each way and his grandfather took him to the 'Old Mission Hut' on Sunday evenings. As a teenager, Jack found Sunday school dull and instead began to roam the streets with other local lads, gradually drifting away from godly influences and interests. Jack had firmly set his sights on a life of living for himself and emptied himself of any thought of God.

Into the Army

Jack wasted no time in 'growing up.' At the age of sixteen he found his way to King's Lynn and, declaring himself to be eighteen, enlisted in the Coldstream Guards. His training as a guardsman was curtailed by the general strike of 1921 and his training squad was sent straight to Chelsea Barracks.

On arriving in his barrack block, Jack was met by the strange scene of a soldier placing a Gospel leaflet on each bed. An Army Scripture Reader, from SASRA, had just been around distributing the tracts and the soldier was mimicking him by collecting up the tracts and redistributing them with hugely exaggerated mannerisms and an extremely sanctimonious expression! Jack had never come across, let alone read, a tract. Despite having turned his back on Christian things, something caused him to rescue one of the tracts from the coal box where it had been thrown. Unscrewing the bit of paper, Jack found a passage of God's Word. As he read it Jack felt something like an electric shock running through him. For the first time he became aware of something being stirred in his heart.

However, Jack became thoroughly involved in regimental life, learnt to drink heavily, and began to smoke 60 cigarettes a day, quickly forgetting the stirring. He also showed an unfortunate natural ability for organising betting and became the battalion bookmaker. For all his natural abilities, Jack was living just the life he had wanted, even though it was a, 'selfish, sinful and commonplace experience.'[55] Mercifully, the 'Captain of our salvation' had other plans for Jack's life that would prove far more exciting and infinitely more worthwhile than the young Guardsman could have imagined.

Service in China

Changes in the political situation on the other side of the world set the scene for this transformation. In 1925, political unrest in China led to the sacking of various British Concessions by Chinese Nationalists. Jack's unit, the Second Battalion, Coldstream Guards, was chosen to go and in January 1927 they embarked on the ship, *Kinfauns Castle*.

As they set sail on their long voyage, the men filled their time by gambling. However, once en route the atmosphere and attitude of the soldiers changed. They began to take life a little more seriously and started a 'swear club,' fining each other a halfpenny each time swore. However, these superficial efforts were not from a real change of heart and had no lasting impact.

The battalion finally arrived in March 1927 and was stationed along Soochow Creek, from where they could take up key positions against the Nationalists within the British Concession. With their arrival the threat to the Concession quickly diminished. Even the Chinese Nationalists' attempts to persuade the British soldiers to kill their officers failed to cause much disruption!

Hallelujah Lizzie

Outside of the Concessions, the threat to Westerners' lives was so great that many missionaries were forced to flee to Shanghai. Certainly, a great number of missionaries were brought across Jack's path. One of his first encounters was with two Salvation Army officers who

News photo of 2nd Battalion Coldstream Guards on their way down to Southampton to embark for China.

arrived at two or three in the morning in a ramshackle old Ford. This vehicle seemed to be held together with bits of string. Nevertheless, 'Hallelujah Lizzie,' as she was affectionately christened, did her job. These young officers took a real interest in the British soldiers, who appreciated their form of practical Christianity. They demonstrated this appreciation by one of the soldiers' engaging the officers in conversation whilst another would walk off with chocolate and fruit from the back of the car. This was all taken in good humour and, while the rest of Shanghai slept, these officers were out winning the souls of the men of the battalion.

Events in the Concession calmed very quickly and in May the battalion busied itself with rehearsals for Trooping the Colour, which took place on 3rd June at Shanghai Race Course. One day as Jack was walking across the barrack square he saw a little man who waved excitedly at him.

'Say, boy! I want a word with you!'

Guardsman Ringer wondered what this strange, little man could possibly want. He was quite the opposite of a guardsman, being short and round, but he was smiling cheerfully and there was a spark in his twinkling eyes. 'I've got a meeting on tonight,' he declared. 'It's a religious meeting, telling all about the Pocket Testament League, and you're coming.'

Jack looked down at this little man and replied, 'Oh, I am, am I?'

However, the man had already dashed off to invite other guardsmen to the meeting. All day Jack could not stop thinking about this poor little man who had no idea what he was letting himself in for. Knowing how much of a 'ribbing' the guardsmen would give him, Jack decided to go along to the meeting just to give him some encouragement.

That evening Jack ambled along pretending to be interested in everything but the meeting, which was being held in a butcher's shop. Finally, after checking that no one was looking, he slipped into the shop and took a seat at the back. There were only a few people there and the little man stood on a box and told them about the Pocket Testament League. As he listened to this unlikely evangelist, Jack again felt an 'electric shock' run through him. He recognised that 'there was some power in this man. He was in touch with reality, with God, and it came home to Jack that night that he needed a Saviour.' A free New Testament was offered and, when no one was looking, Jack took one and dashed away.

A Red Cap

Shortly after, Jack was transferred from the battalion to the Red Caps[56] and became a military policeman. Right beside the Military

Police barracks was a hut built by missionaries as a place for the soldiers to go, where they were given something to eat, a cup of tea, and a quiet corner where they could study the Bible. Will Webb, a missionary of the China Inland Mission, led a Bible study there every night.

Jack was billeted nearby and was able to pop in for a cup of tea as often as he liked. He took advantage of the free brew but was also drawn by an attractive quality, a 'mysterious something,' that the missionaries had. Jack became increasingly aware that they were in possession of something vitally important that he utterly lacked. Despite having lived exactly as he had wanted, he had found no joy, peace, or fulfilment. He had given himself to one bad habit after another but they only served to make him more aware of how great was the burden of sin that he carried.

Contact with these Christians made Jack more miserable, as their evident purity and deep peace showed that they were right with God and he was not. He increased his efforts to reform himself, but to no avail. At every service he attended something else would 'pierce his heart.' He was convinced that someone had told the speaker his personal history. He became increasingly distressed at his sin and disillusioned with his ability to escape from it. He began to think that he was living in a world full of 'mad prisoners' from which only a select few seemed to have been freed to live unaffected by their surroundings. Many times he thought about suicide and wished that he would be shot and killed.

Substitutions

Around this time Jack was on duty at a road junction with another soldier. They had been discussing life and all its problems and had reached a lull in the conversation when Jack suddenly fainted and slid to the ground. His fellow guard picked him up, put him in a rickshaw, and sent him to the Medical Centre. By the time he had arrived at the medical centre he felt better but the doctor who assessed him ordered him to be bedded down.

The following morning, in accordance with orders, he attended the sick parade. Jack was proud of the fact that he had never been sick during his whole army career and he had no intention of starting now. He tried his best to convince the medical officer that he was 'fighting fit;' however, the doctor insisted that Jack rest for another day. Another man took Jack's place on duty.

That night a quarrel broke out between some English soldiers and Portuguese sailors, and the Red Caps and the Chinese police were called. The Chinese police began firing their rifles in the ballroom, causing everyone to run for cover. In all the confusion, Jack's substitute was stabbed in the back and died a week later.

It did not escape Jack's notice that, only a fortnight before his death, this man, his substitute, had accepted Christ as his own personal Saviour. Jack, who longed to die, was spared, whilst instead this man had died and was now with his Lord and Saviour. Jack would never forget the moment he looked into the grave of the man who had been killed in his place.

After a few more days of wrestling with himself, Jack knew that he had to make a decision one way or the other: to follow the example of the missionaries or to try to drown himself in the life that had previously brought no peace or relief. He decided to ask the man in charge of the hut to show him the way to God. As he talked and told the man of his great inner turmoil, the missionary's big, brotherly hand reached over and patted his head.

Laddie, you're carrying a load that none of us can carry. It is too big for you, and the sooner you drop it the better. You are trying to bear the load of your sin, which only One can do, and His name is the Lord Jesus. He went to the Cross and suffered indescribable agony for you: He took your place and died the death which was really yours: He waits for you to accept Him by faith as your Sin-bearer, Saviour and Sovereign.

He then asked Jack to kneel down and simply accept the Lord Jesus as his Saviour. Jack knelt on the floor, longing for this peace from the guilt of sin and to be given a fresh start as a new creation in Christ. However, as he knelt he could not bring himself to pray. Finally he threw himself on the mercy of God and cried, 'God be merciful to me, a sinner!' The battle was won! Jack Ringer had 'passed from death to life; from the power of Satan to God; all things had become new; and the load was gone.'

The following day, Jack read his Bible in the barrack room. He was in no doubt that a miracle had happened. For the first time he had a quiet assurance. He realised that he had indeed been reconciled to God through Jesus Christ. The transformation was not apparent to Jack alone. Without his even saying a word, it was clear to all that he was an utterly changed man.

That evening brought a natural opportunity to 'nail his colours to the mast' and confess Christ publicly. The soldier in the bed opposite Jack's made a pointed remark, causing him to blush with shame. By God's grace, Jack opened his mouth and the Lord literally put words into it and so, 'as far as that barrack room was concerned, his [bridges] were burned behind him.'

Discipleship

Jack continued to tell others about what God had done in his life. He wrote letters to all of his friends and family back in Britain and the following six months were a time of real blessing, discipleship, and spiritual growth. He was nurtured by good, regular Bible studies and Christian fellowship. Through these God opened his eyes to a greater understanding of the Lord Jesus Christ and Jack began to feel a definite calling from God to undertake some special service.

The news that the battalion bookmaker had become a 'Bible Puncher' spread rapidly. One by one, his old companions came to see him. Jack expected to be mocked by his old friends but instead they encouraged him saying, 'well done, Jack, if we had the gumption we would do the same.' Later, Jack was blessed to see a few of them turning to the Lord.

Conversions in the 'Hell Hole'

Six months after Jack's transformation, the battalion left China for Britain. As there was no Chaplain on the ship, five of the soldiers asked permission from the Adjutant to use the hammock room in the bowels of the ship for prayer and Bible study.

They started with five in Hong Kong; they finished with fifty. Before embarking, a missionary had managed to get a case of hymn books and tracts onto the ship. This helped greatly with the effectiveness of these meetings.

Having been a Christian for six months, Jack was elected leader and so he gave the Bible studies. He had been intensively studying the Epistle to the Romans for the past six months under the guidance of Will Webb and the men received the benefit of those first thrilling steps in God's Word.

This compartment at the bottom of the ship was so hot that it was nicknamed 'the Hell Hole.' Despite this nickname, a heavenly work was done there and a number of men were converted. However, this is not the whole story: behind this small band of enthusiastic young Christians were a thousand praying missionaries back in China. As a result of the continuing conflict the missionaries were evacuated to Shanghai where they took great interest in this particular ship and prayed earnestly for a work of the Spirit of God to be done amongst these men.

Jack arrived back in Britain on 21st March 1928 and the clear blessings of God upon the voyage confirmed his thoughts that God was calling him to some special service. However, he knew that he must first have a firm foundation in God's Word.

Preparation

Five years previously, Will Webb and a friend had attended a Bible study group in Swindon. They had heard that young men had been 'getting religion' through the ministry of another young man and decided to go along and disrupt the meeting for a joke. This spectacularly backfired, as a strange restraint fell upon them so that they could only sit and listen. When the leader (Richard Ewings) spoke, all their arguments disintegrated and finally they knelt together and yielded their lives to the Lord. After Jack left the army, on Will Webb's recommendation he visited Richard Ewings. After a month's trial assisting him, Jack was invited to stay on indefinitely under Ewings's supervision.

Through this 'apprenticeship,' Jack received thorough Bible teaching and training in practical Christian work, including running a Sunday school, Bible classes, 'Lantern Lectures,'[57] and conference ministry. Despite leaving the army, Jack's military service was far from over and he was appointed as a part-time Army Scripture Reader with SASRA for the Depot of the Wiltshire Regiment at Devizes.

Jack had read all about George Müller, who built many homes for orphans in Bristol trusting only in the Lord for provision and living by faith in God. At his Bible study groups, Jack tried to interest the teenagers in 'faith missions' in the hope that they would hear the call of God to take the Gospel overseas. None was interested in this calling, but the more Jack sought to persuade others, the more it became clear that the Lord was calling him. However, now aged 34, Jack felt that he was too old.

Called to the Frontier

Brigadier-General FD Frost was a Christian who had earned his pension in the Indian Army and felt he owed it to the Indians to spend his retirement in evangelising them.[58] Having had some experience with the Pashtun people, he felt led to work amongst them in the North-West Frontier region.

General Frost happened to visit Swindon and explained that he needed ex-soldiers to work amongst such a martial people. As he sat in the meeting that night and heard this call, Jack felt that God was speaking directly to him. The call was so clear that he immediately told the General that he was willing to go. After the meeting Jack was privileged to lead someone to Christ. Taking this as an endorsement of his decision, he applied to the organisation to which the General belonged, the 'Central Asian Mission.'

Jack had left the army with £30. God had indeed provided all his needs, just as He had for George Müller, and after ten years Jack still had £30. As his train left Swindon station in the first stage of his long journey to India, he gave an envelope to Richard Ewings containing the £30, a note of thanks, and a request that the money be used to bring someone else on in the faith.

Jack arrived in Bombay on 11th November 1938. He made his way up-country to join General Frost in the Mardan area of the North-West Frontier Province of what is now Pakistan. He threw himself into learning the Pashto language of the Pashtun people, the ethnic group spanning the border between Pakistan and Afghanistan, and remained as a missionary for the next four decades.

The young Jack Ringer, battalion bookmaker, had set out on a life in pursuit of earthly treasure and human pleasure and found only emptiness. God rescued him from this and made him into a good soldier of Jesus Christ with the certain hope of heaven and a burning concern for the lost. As Jack wrote, 'The time for evangelisation is now... The cost is blood and tears. The rewards are incorruptible crowns.'

Jack Ringer's full account is contained in his biography, LT Daniel, *Frontier Challenge: There Was a Man Sent from God, Whose Name Was John – Biography of John Ringer, 1904–85*, Sheffield, Bridge Publications, 1987.

15

Duncan Campbell's Personal Testimony

From the Trenches to the Pulpit
1898–1972

Edited by Philip Bray

Duncan Campbell is best known for the mighty work that God performed through him in the Christian Revival on the Isle of Lewis in the Outer Hebrides, Scotland from 1949 to 1952. He was invited by a local minister to visit the Isle of Lewis for a ten-day mission. He remained for three years. Many of the young men who had served in the Second World War had returned to a spiritual vacuum, confused and troubled by what they had experienced. Most had turned away from their Christian upbringing. Campbell saw such men turn back to God, experiencing a revival that shook the whole of Lewis and which has been immortalised in the annals of Christian history. Since that time there has not been a revival like it in Britain.

However, Duncan Campbell's first profession after his conversion was as an infantry soldier in the Argyll and Sutherland Highlanders, a Regiment of the British Army. God had prepared Campbell on the battlefields of the First World War for a powerful and effective Christian ministry that was to last for decades. After being discharged from the military he worked for the Faith Mission and over a period of 23 years with the United Free Church of Scotland in three different parishes. His simple conviction was that if God could save *him*, God could save anyone. Without higher education or theological training, Campbell became a minister of the Gospel, understanding that the power to transform lives was not a human gift or aptitude, but a spiritual work of God that accompanied the faithful preaching of the Gospel.

This chapter, abridged from his own words with the kind permission of his family, recounts how the revival preacher of the Isle of Lewis came to a personal knowledge of Christ, was preserved spiritually and physically through the horrors of the trenches of the First World War, and was then called into Christian ministry.

* * *

The Greatest Discovery and Enlistment

I was a piper, playing and dancing at a concert in 1913, when suddenly God spoke to me. I had a praying mother and a praying father and I believe that they were deeply burdened that night because I had gone to the dance. While I was playing a Scottish tune called 'The Green Hills of Tyrol,' God spoke to me. My fingers continued to play, but my soul was frightfully disturbed, and I found myself dwelling not on the Green Hills of Tyrol but on the Green Hill of Calvary. I was so disturbed that, when I had finished playing the song, I stepped off the stage, went to the chairman, and said that I would be leaving the concert. He looked at me and asked 'are you well?' I said, 'Yes, very well in body, but fearfully disturbed in my mind. I have just made a discovery that I am on the way to hell.' The chairman was a minister (I regret having to say that) and he looked at me and said, 'You'll soon get over that.' I am thankful to God that I have not 'got over it' to this day.

On my way home, I passed a church and to my amazement I found it still lit at eleven o'clock at night. I could not understand it. Of course, I had been away from home on business and I did not know that two pilgrims from the Faith Mission were conducting a mission in the parish and here they were still in the church at eleven o'clock. I listened at the door and heard someone praying. Who should it be but my own father, pouring out his heart for the parish and for his own family! Oh, God bless such fathers! Horses could not have dragged me past that meeting. I went in, still dressed in my piper's regalia, carrying a set of bagpipes and two swords that I had been using to demonstrate sword dancing. I left the bagpipes and the swords on the back seat of the church, walked up the aisle, and sat down beside my father. He looked at me and said, 'I am glad to see you here, boy. I am glad to see you here.'

After a few minutes, one of the sisters who spoke our language (Gaelic) rose and read a text of Scripture. 'Indeed God speaks once, or twice, yet no one notices it.'[59] I knew that God was speaking to me, but I was so afraid of disturbing the meeting that I rose to leave. However, as I walked out I fell on my knees not once but half a dozen times. I was so distressed in my soul that I was afraid that the very ground would open and I would fall into hell as I came under conviction of the Holy Ghost.

When I did leave, I remained deeply troubled and must have

fallen on my knees and prayed six more times on my way home. I did not arrive home until after two o'clock in the morning and I found my dear mother on her knees by the kitchen fire. She had not been able to attend the prayer meeting that night as some members of the family had come to stay who needed to be looked after. I told her what had happened to me and of my distress. She looked at me and said, 'Your cousins are in your bedroom but I shall soon get a bed ready for you. But I would say this to you, my boy;' (I was just in my teens), 'go out to the barn and tell God what you have just told me.'

I can still see the straw, prepared for the horses in the morning, where I fell on my knees. To this day I remember the prayer that I offered: 'God, I know not how to come, I know not what to do, but my God I am coming now. Oh, have mercy upon me.' In less time than it takes me to recount the story, God had swept into my life and I was gloriously born again. A miracle had taken place. After all, is it not true that a born-again Christian is a supernatural being, a supernatural being who has had a supernatural experience? Blessed be God! Since that day I have not had one occasion to doubt the work that God performed in my heart. It was real, it was definite, and, blessed be God, it was supernatural. Shortly afterwards I enlisted in the Army at the outbreak of the First World War.

Battles Within and Without

I had not been in the Forces for very long when I discovered that there were dangers living within me that were more than a match for me. I am thankful to God that He kept me from open sin. Oh, how I praise Him for that! I also had a sense of His gracious presence in the trenches and I knew Him there, but I was still troubled by 'indwelling sin.' It was an enemy in the garrison of my soul fighting against God. Again and again it brought me into bondage. I often fell on my knees in the trenches and asked God to forgive me for the thoughts of my heart, which sometimes were not too clean. I was terribly conscious of the truth that 'the heart is more deceitful than all else and is desperately sick; Who can understand it?'[60] Then a remarkable thing happened; the second outstanding experience of my life.

Somehow, someone in authority found out that I was a farmer's son and that consequently I knew something about horses. I was immediately transferred out of the infantry into the Cavalry Corps. Oh, God's ways are wonderful! It was because I was transferred to the cavalry that God met with me for the second time.

While taking part in the last major charge of the British cavalry at Amiens on 12th April 1918, I was severely wounded and was thrown onto the ground, where I lay next to a dead horse. My own horse rolled onto me, injuring my spine. I was bleeding heavily from other wounds. As I lay there the blood flowed out of me and I was convinced that I was dying. As these thoughts coursed through my mind, suddenly a verse of Scripture came to me: 'and holiness, without which no man can see God.'[61] Even in the deep and glorious knowledge that I was born again, I felt very unworthy and unfit to meet God. Then, in the providence of God, another remarkable thing happened.

Lord Strathcona's Horse (Royal Canadians), known as the 'Canadian Horse,' were ordered to continue the advance. As they charged over the bloody battlefield, covered with hundreds of wounded and dying men, a hoof struck me in the spine. I must have groaned in pain and that groan registered in the mind of the rider. When the charge was over he was one of the few that came back and I tell you that there were very few. It was a dreadful day. However, he came right back to where I lay, dismounted, lifted me up, threw me across his horse's back, and galloped to the nearest casualty clearing station. It was on that horse's back that the glorious miracle happened.

I remembered a prayer by Murray M'Cheyne which my father used to pray and I cried to God, 'God, oh God, make me as holy as a saved sinner can be.' God did it. God swept into my life and I knew in a matter of minutes an experience that I did not think was possible this side of heaven. His waters flowed throughout my soul and inner being and I was healed, not physically, but spiritually. A sense of God flowed through me and at that moment I felt as pure as an angel. Do not misunderstand me: only God could know my true state, but that was how I felt.

At that time I could barely speak a word of English. I spoke Gaelic, the language of the Highlands of Scotland. I could not praise God in English; I could not pray in English. I read and sang in Gaelic. I was too weak through loss of blood to sing that afternoon, but I could repeat the Psalms. As I lay in the station, I repeated over and over in Gaelic the Scottish Psalm:

British cavalry await orders to move forward during operations in the Arras region, 1917.

O thou my soul, bless God the Lord
and all that in me is,
be stirred up [by] His Holy Name
to magnify and to bless.

Not one person in that casualty clearing station could understand a single word of what I said, but God came in convincing power and within an hour seven Canadians had been saved. It was my first experience of a 'Holy Ghost revival.'

I had not been there for very long when I was evacuated back to Scotland for further treatment. I remained in hospital for eleven months more and there experienced the gracious moving of God. There was nothing more wonderful than to see God working and saving men and women. I could not preach much, but just a word about the Lord Jesus Christ did it! After a year and one month I was sent back home to the farm and demobilised.

From Military to Christian Service

I was now more or less fully recovered from my injuries and my parents were very keen for me to enter Christian ministry. However, what university or college would accept me with my very limited English? I immediately came to the conclusion that it was not necessary. Why should I spend five to seven years in training when God in a matter of minutes could send revival? Therefore, with the permission of my parents, I just went out to the villages of Argyll in Scotland and preached. In a matter of days I saw what is commonly referred to as 'the Mid-Argyll Revival.' The burden of my message was simple: 'He saved me and because He saved a sinner like me, He can save you.' For five years a young brother from Ireland and I saw the Hand of God in revival. I think I could trace it back to that experience on the horse's back when God blessed me again.

God's Arm is not shortened, His Ear is not heavy, and the God that did it for me is no respecter of persons; the God that did it for me can do it for you, now.

Epilogue

The Unwritten Chapter

It is a long tradition of the British Army that when a regiment takes part in a battle, it is awarded a 'Battle Honour' by the reigning monarch. The names of these honours are then embroidered and displayed on each regiment's colours. One regiment, *The Rifles*, carries its honours not on colours, but on its belt buckle. When the regiment was formed it was decided that one space on the buckle would be left blank for future honours. So it is with this book.

There are doubtless many other accounts that could have been included but, through the restrictions of space or plain ignorance of the editors, are not included. However, this last chapter is subtitled 'The Unwritten Chapter' as it is the desire of the editors and authors that the accounts of this book might encourage every reader personally to trust and serve the Lord Jesus Christ with all their heart and strength, and so to write this 'Unwritten Chapter.'

Notes

[1] 1 Timothy 2:1–2.

[2] Matthew 26:39.

[3] Philippians 4:7.

[4] All quotes, unless otherwise stated, are taken from P Doddridge, *The Life of the Hon. Colonel Gardiner: Who Was Slain at the Battle of Prestonpans*, Edinburgh, Mundell, Doig, and Stevenson, 1807.

[5] A former rank in the British Army; one rank above Lieutenant, and one below Captain.

[6] Romans 3:24–5, King James version (KJV).

[7] [in other words, enough momentum to allow control]

[8] Acts 27:24.

[9] All quotes, unless otherwise stated, are taken from A Crichton, *The Life and Diary of Lt Col J Blackadder of the Cameronian Regiment and Deputy Governor of Stirling Castle*, London, W Baynes and Sons, 1824.

[10] Ecclesiastes 1:9.

[11] A period of persecution that resulted from an attempt to extend the Church of England's authority from 1660. As a result many ministers took to preaching in the open fields, and not in buildings, hence the title, 'field preachers.'

[12] 1 Samuel 7:12.

[13] WS Churchill, *Marlborough, His Life and Times,* Chicago, University of Chicago Press, 2002). Reproduced with permission of Curtis Brown, London on behalf of the Estate of Sir Winston Churchill. Copyright © Winston S. Churchill.

[14] Psalm 103:1.

[15] The outer wall of a ditch in a fortification.

[16] 1 Corinthians 2:2.

[17] 2 Corinthians 1:12.

[18] Hebrews 12:14, KJV.

[19] Titus 2:12.

[20] This rebellion, also known as India's First War of Independence, began in May 1857. The uprising lasted until 20th June 1858.

[21] All quotations in this chapter are taken from CH Malan, *A Soldier's Experience of God's Love and of His Faithfulness To His Word,* London, James Nisbet & Co., 1874.

[22] Haggai 2:4.

[23] James 5:17.

[24] 2 Kings 2:14.

[25] 1 Samuel 3:18.

[26] Psalm 119:31.

[27] [Not the Colonel James Gardner featured in Chapter 3 who died at the Battle of Prestonpans in 1745.]

[28] [Vulgar, lewdly humorous language or joking.]

[29] The present writer's great great uncle. Afterwards a Field Marshal.

[30] Psalm 91:9–11.

[31] Puttee: cloth tightly wound round the leg for support and protection.

[32] Romans 8:28.

[33] Proverbs 3:26, KJV.

[34] Philippians 1:23.

[35] 2 Timothy 2:4.

[36] All quotes are taken from Reverend Lovell Pocock, *With Those in Peril: A Chaplain's Life in the Royal Navy*, Upton-upon-Severn, Reverend Lovell Pocock in association with the Self Publishing Association Ltd, 1989.

[37] 1 Timothy 1:15.

[38] Hebrews 12:2.

[39] 2 Corinthians 9:15.

[40] 2 Corinthians 4:4.

[41] 2 Corinthians 11:25–26.

[42] Matthew 24:13.

[43] Matthew 6:33.

[44] Philippians 1:21.

[45] 1 John 3:2.

[46] Psalm 78:1–4.

[47] Minesweepers were primarily used as security for convoys in order to protect cargo ships and dispose of any mines. They had a high casualty rate, with 63 of the 140 ships of our kind being destroyed, one of which was the *M435* on which I served.

[48] Psalm 50:15.

[49] Psalm 91:7.

[50] A gasometer is a large, expandable metal structure, in which domestic gas is stored.

[51] The telescopic walls that rise and fall as the gasometer is filled with or emptied of gas.

[52] Psalm 139:1 and 8.

[53] John 1:2–3 and John 1:11–12.

[54] Matthew 1:23.

[55] All quotes are taken from LT Daniel, *Frontier Challenge: There Was a Man Sent from God, Whose Name Was John – Biography of John Ringer, 1904–85*, Sheffield, Bridge Publications, 1987.

[56] The British Army's military police, so named due to their distinctive red caps.

[57] A presentation using projected images.

[58] He was also the father of John Frost, later Major General John Frost, CB DSO MC, who most famously commanded 2nd Battalion, the Parachute Regiment at Arnhem, immortalised in the film *A Bridge too Far.*

[59] Job 33:14.

[60] Jeremiah 17:9.

[61] Hebrews 12:14, KJV.